Gangs

OPPOSING
VIEWPOINTS®
DIGESTS

Gangs

GAIL B. STEWART

Greenhaven Press Inc., San Diego, California

Library of Congress Cataloging-in-Publication Data

Stewart, Gail, 1949–
    Gangs / Gail B. Stewart.
        p.   cm. — (Opposing viewpoints digests)
    Includes bibliographical references and index.
    Summary: Presents contrasting viewpoints on the following questions: "How serious a problem are gangs in the United States?" "What factors encourage gang behavior?" and "How can gangs be eliminated?"
    ISBN 1-56510-751-9 (lib. : alk. paper). — ISBN 1-56510-750-0 (pbk. : alk. paper)
    1. Gangs—United States—Juvenile literature.   2. Gangs—Government policy—United States—Juvenile literature.   3. Violent crimes—United States—Juvenile literature.   4. Crime prevention—United States—Juvenile literature.   [1. Gangs.]   I. Title.   II. Series.
HV6439.U5S77   1998
364.36—DC21   97-40096
                                                                              CIP
                                                                               AC

Cover Photo: Donna DeCesare/Impact Visuals
AP Photo: 42 (Andrew Sullivan), 87 (Rene Macura)
© Donna DeCesare/Impact Visuals: 30, 55
Natasha Frost: 19
Library of Congress: 11, 13, 15
Photofest: 33
© Richard Renaldi/Impact Visuals: 51

©1998 by Greenhaven Press, Inc.
PO Box 289009, San Diego, CA 92198-9009

Printed in the U.S.A.

CONTENTS

FOREWORD

"The only way in which a human being can make some approach to knowing the whole of a subject is by hearing what can be said about it by persons of every variety of opinion and studying all modes in which it can be looked at by every character of mind. No wise man ever acquired his wisdom in any mode but this."

—John Stuart Mill

Today, young adults are inundated with a wide variety of points of view on an equally wide spectrum of subjects. Often overshadowing traditional books and newspapers as forums for these views are a host of broadcast, print, and electronic media, including television news and entertainment programs, talk shows, and commercials; radio talk shows and call-in lines; movies, home videos, and compact discs; magazines and supermarket tabloids; and the increasingly popular and influential Internet.

For teenagers, this multiplicity of sources, ideas, and opinions can be both positive and negative. On the one hand, a wealth of useful, interesting, and enlightening information is readily available virtually at their fingertips, underscoring the need for teens to recognize and consider a wide range of views besides their own. As Mark Twain put it, "It were not best that we should all think alike; it is difference of opinion that makes horse races." On the other hand, the range of opinions on a given subject is often too wide to absorb and analyze easily. Trying to keep up with, sort out, and form personal opinions from such a barrage can be daunting for anyone, let alone young people who have not yet acquired effective critical judgment skills.

Moreover, to the task of evaluating this assortment of impersonal information, many teenagers bring firsthand experience of serious and emotionally charged social and health problems, including divorce, family violence, alcoholism and drug abuse, rape, unwanted pregnancy, the spread of AIDS, and eating disorders. Teens are often forced to deal with these problems before they are capable of objective opinion based on reason and judgment. All too often, teens' response to these deep personal issues is impulsive rather than carefully considered.

Greenhaven Press's Opposing Viewpoints Digests are designed to aid in examining important current issues in a way that develops critical thinking and evaluating skills. Each book presents thought-provoking argument and stimulating debate on a single issue. By examining an issue from many different points of view, readers come to realize its complexity and acknowledge the validity of opposing opinions. This insight is especially helpful in writing reports, research papers, and persuasive essays, when students must competently address common objections and controversies related to their topic. In addition, examination of the diverse mix of opinions in each volume challenges readers to question their own strongly held opinions and assumptions. While the point of such examination is not to change readers' minds, examining views that oppose their own will certainly deepen their own knowledge of the issue and help them realize exactly why they hold the opinion they do.

The Opposing Viewpoint Digests offer a number of unique features that sharpen young readers' critical thinking and reading skills. To assure an appropriate and consistent reading level for young adults, all essays in each volume are written by a single author. Each essay heavily quotes readable primary sources that are fully cited to allow for further research and documentation. Thus, primary sources are introduced in a context to enhance comprehension.

In addition, each volume includes extensive research tools. A section containing relevant source material includes interviews, excerpts from original research, and the opinions of prominent spokespersons. A "facts about" section allows students to peruse relevant facts and statistics; these statistics are also fully cited, allowing students to question and analyze the credibility of the source. Two bibliographies, one for young adults and one listing the author's sources, are also included; both are annotated to guide student research. Finally, a comprehensive index allows students to scan and locate content efficiently.

Greenhaven's Opposing Viewpoints Digests, like Greenhaven's higher level and critically acclaimed Opposing Viewpoints Series, have been developed around the concept that an awareness and appreciation for the complexity of seemingly simple issues is particularly important in a democratic society. In a democracy, the common good is often, and very appropriately, decided by open debate of widely varying views. As one of our democracy's greatest advocates, Thomas Jefferson, observed, "Difference of opinion leads to inquiry, and inquiry to truth." It is to this principle that Opposing Viewpoints Digests are dedicated.

"Today's gangs are urban terrorists. Heavily armed and more violent than ever before, . . . [g]ang members are turning our streets and neighborhoods into war zones."

A Concise Look at Gangs

It does not seem to matter in what part of the United States one lives; in cities large and small, in urban, suburban, and rural settings, the idea of "gang" conveys an image we all recognize. If we have never met an actual gang member, we have seen them on television, we have heard the rap music associated with gangs, the lyrics of which many deplore for violent and sexist content. We have seen the block-letter graffiti with which gangs mark their turf on walls and garbage dumpsters. We have seen young people not affiliated with a gang dress like gang members anyway, pants sagging, hats cocked to one side or the other, colorful bandannas precisely knotted.

The evidence of gang violence is well documented and pervasive, as well. We hear about the drug dealing and the assaults. We read about the lives cut short, the drive-by shootings, the innocent people gunned down in the line of fire. The presence of gangs in our communities is frightening because of the crime and violence that seem to surround gang members and activities.

The crime statistics are grim and getting grimmer. In Los Angeles County, California, for example, gang-related homicides for the period January through June doubled between

1989 and 1990. The victims of these homicides were young—of the six hundred gang-related murders in 1990, the average age of the victim was twenty-one. This reflects a new trend in crime statistics—although the *overall* crime rate appears to be going down, the violent crime rate among juveniles is increasing, especially the homicide rate. For instance, one criminologist studied the crime statistics for Boston, Massachusetts, and found that in the ten years between 1985 and 1995, the murder rate among fourteen- to fifteen-year-olds had soared 165 percent. Among white teens, the murder rate had doubled; among African Americans it had tripled. Though not a factor in all of these murders, gang violence was responsible for many—primarily, say experts, because of gang members' easy access to lethal weapons.

"Gangs hold many neighborhoods hostage," one federal newsletter reports.

> Residents are fearful of leaving their homes. They are afraid to let their children play in area parks that have been taken over by gangs for drug dealing. Neighborhood businesses suffer economically because residents are hesitant to leave their homes to shop. And community services, such as law enforcement and courts, find themselves with escalating costs as they struggle to deal with gangs.[1]

A final report by the California State Task Force on Gangs and Drugs in 1991 concurred:

> Today's gangs are urban terrorists. Heavily armed and more violent than ever before, they are quick to use terror and intimidation to seize and protect their share of the lucrative drug market. Gang members are turning our streets and neighborhoods into war zones, where it takes an act of courage simply to walk to the corner store.[2]

Although experts agree that the violence associated with gangs has increased dramatically in recent years, the problem of gangs in the United States is nothing new. Quite the contrary; criminal gangs made up of juveniles have existed since the early nineteenth century, arising out of the poorest immigrant neighborhoods of the East Coast.

New York City was home to the first American gangs, simply because it was, for European immigrants at that time, the primary entrance point to the New World. New York, a bustling city in 1810, was not prepared to absorb the thousands of people arriving from the ports of Europe every week. But instead of moving on to settle elsewhere, most immigrants opted to remain in the only parts of the city where they could afford a room, the poorest and, as more and more people arrived, the most overcrowded.

The Five Points district of Manhattan, home to a great many immigrants of the era, is a case in point. The district was a relatively low- to middle-income residential area until about 1820, when the first wave of Irish immigrants settled there. Like other groups who came after them, the Irish were hoping for a better, more prosperous life for their families, including land and small business ownership. In the meantime, they endured life in Five Points. New Irish arrivals settled there, too, glad at least to be living with countrymen with whom they shared a language, customs, and religion.

The dream of owning property—or for that matter of finding a good job—faded for most of these immigrants. Most were uneducated and unskilled rural folk, ready to work but competing for too few jobs at low pay. As a result, Five Points became a dead end for the poorest Irish immigrants, and the area became notorious for its filth, its disease, and its squalor.

Roach Guards, Dead Rabbits, and True Blue Americans

Breeding grounds not only for poverty, the slum of Five Points and other overcrowded immigrant areas became the

Immigration, overpopulation, and a scarcity of jobs caused widespread poverty in nineteenth-century New York City.

first "hoods," giving rise to the first notorious youth gangs. In Five Points, boys in their teens or older often organized themselves into gangs, both in defense (there was great prejudice against these Irish immigrants) and as a way of making money illegally—through pickpocketing, theft, and extortion from neighborhood businesses. Some of the gangs numbered in the hundreds; at least one had over a thousand members.

The gangs had strange-sounding names, such as the Roach Guards, the True Blue Americans, and the Plug Uglies. The Dead Rabbits, another gang in the area, were so named because when they advanced into a fight with another gang, they carried poles impaling the bodies of dead rabbits. The gangs wore colorful costumes, says historian James Haskins, and usually fought in their undershirts. "The Roach Guards wore a blue stripe on their pantaloons, the Dead Rabbits a red stripe. . . . The True Blue Americans wore stovepipe hats and ankle-length frock coats."[3]

In addition to adopting signature colors, the gangs of the nineteenth century started other rituals that are associated with street gangs of today. For instance, just as today's gang members give each other nicknames like "Shorty" and "Killer-G," the Irish gang members christened one another with names like "Little Red" and "Toothless Mike." They also originated the requirement that prospective gang members fight their way into a gang as an initiation.

Various Gang Activity

Early street gang activity was somewhat specialized. Some gangs devoted their time exclusively to petty crime—random mugging, stealing, and con games. Taken to extremes, the Plug Uglies thought nothing of injuring or murdering citizens. According to one researcher, "One Plug Ugly was reported to have cracked a stranger's spine in three places in order to win a two-dollar bet."[4]

Other gangs became hired thugs for unions or various political organizations in the city. By 1855, more than thirty thousand young men in New York City owed allegiance to gang leaders and through them to various political machines. When it came time to turn out the vote, intimidate a candidate giving a public speech, or disrupt a workers strike, the gangs were often called upon.

But perhaps the activity for which the early gangs were best known was brawling among themselves. One of the fiercest rivalries in New York was between the Bowery Boys, who came from a poor working-class area near Five Points and the Dead Rabbits, whose members were unemployed, like most of the residents in Five Points.

Gang members fought with ice picks, bats, knives, and muskets—not as sophisticated as today's Uzis, but just as deadly.

The brawls between rival gangs were often long, bloody wars. For three decades, in fact, between the 1830s and the 1860s, some gangs' fights were so common and so numerous, says one historian, that "hardly a week passed that the Dead Rabbits . . . did not engage in battle. Sometimes these battles lasted two or three days [with] endless melees of beating, maiming, and murder. . . . Regiments of soldiers in full battle dress, marching through the streets to the scene of a gang melee, were not an uncommon sight."[5]

Overcrowded immigrant areas in several eastern cities gave rise to the first youth gangs.

The Spread of Gangs

By the mid–nineteenth century, gangs had spread to poor sections of other eastern cities. Philadelphia, in particular, was home to at least fifty-two different gangs between 1836 and 1878. Stuart Blumin, a reporter for the *New York Tribune*, described the northern suburbs of Philadelphia in 1848 and 1849 as filled with "loafers who brave only gangs, herd together in squads," and write their gangs' names "in chalk or charcoal on every dead-wall, fence and stable-door."[6]

Immigration boomed in the years following the Civil War, and from places other than Ireland. People from eastern and southern Europe settled, as the Irish had, in poor sections of the cities of the East. The adolescent and young adult males who joined in gang activity had as many reasons as their Irish predecessors. By the early twentieth century, sociologist Irving A. Spergel writes,

> Gangs fulfilled a range of functions for marginal youths, in addition to protecting local turf, fighting, thieving, partying, and teaching how to survive and adapt in the new urban environment. They helped politicians to get the vote out and intimidated opposition candidates. Young toughs assisted both union leaders and factory workers to protect their respective interests."[7]

New Immigrants, New Gangs

America's development from an agrarian to an industrial society underlays the formation of African American and Latino gangs in the twentieth century. In the decades between 1900 and 1930, industrial cities experienced a ballooning population as low-income farmworkers from the southern and southwestern states—most of whom were black or Latino—headed north and west, lured by the promise of factory jobs in the cities. Strict new laws restricting European immigration had slowed the supply of low-wage workers, and black and Latino workers filled the void.

Early gangs had strange-sounding names and wore distinctive clothing and colors. Pictured is the Short Tail Gang loitering under a New York pier.

But the swelling population had the same negative effects in Chicago, Detroit, Cleveland, and Los Angeles as it had in New York a century before. More people in the low-income sections of urban areas meant overcrowding, deteriorating conditions, poverty—and gangs. By the mid-1920s it was estimated that more than thirteen hundred gangs operated in Chicago alone, many Latino and African American. In Los Angeles, the most powerful gang in 1920 was a black gang called the Boozies, who routinely fought several Latino gangs over territory.

Beginning in the 1940s and 1950s, new gangs vied for superiority in Los Angeles, with names such as the Businessmen, the Home Street Gang, the Slauson Gang, and the Neighborhood Gang. Near Chicago, the Vice Lords, one of the largest of that city's gangs, was formed in St. Charles at the Illinois State Training School for Boys. Boys released from this reform school returned to their Chicago neighborhoods and soon organized an intimidating force.

The rise of the modern gang was taking place on the West Coast, too. Sometime between the late 1960s and early 1970s, the gang known as the Crips was formed in Los Angeles at Washington High School. Members adopted blue as their gang color, supposedly because it was one of the school's colors, to set them apart from other gangs. The Piru Gang also appeared about this time, named after Piru Street, where most of its members lived. Eventually the Pirus became known as the Bloods, known as the biggest rivals of the Crips gang.

Gangs Today

There have been changes in the ways gangs operate, most notably in the ways gangs make money. Gangs today control a large share of the drug market; as low-cost crack cocaine became the drug of choice in the most run-down urban neighborhoods, gangs eagerly took up the role of distributor.

"On any city block, in any bar or pool hall, any of the apartment buildings and projects in the inner city, there are the sellers," says one youth counselor from Detroit. "The kids can be as young as nine or ten; all they have to do is hand over a little bag and hold on to the money. Every hour or so an overseer comes and takes the money, makes sure the dealer has more crack to sell if he needs it, and the whole things starts over again."[8]

It seems that there is no limit to the amount of money to be made in the selling and distribution of drugs, primarily because the supply of customers is endless. In 1996 the Gangster Disciples gang in Chicago made an estimated $500 million from selling crack and cocaine, under the leadership of a convict named Larry Hoover, already serving a life sentence. In California investigators say that the Bloods and the Crips gangs together have cornered more than 35 percent of the national drug market.

Megaviolence

One does not have to be a crack or cocaine user to encounter gang violence, however. Gangs' destructive activity affects every community in which they are present, and is inextricably linked to the ready availability of weapons to young gang members.

Many residents of gang-infested neighborhoods agree that much of the violence has nothing to do with drug deals. It might erupt over a car, a girl, or even the wrong color bandanna in the wrong neighborhood—but what might have been a dangerous fight years ago is lethal today. One man who until recently was involved with a California gang described one gang feud that escalated in the last five years from a drunken party brawl into a series of deadly drive-bys.

Source: Office of Juvenile Justice and Delinquency Prevention

States Reporting the Most Gang Members

In ascending order

1. California
2. Texas
3. Illinois
4. Colorado
5. Arizona
6. Florida
7. Missouri
8. Washington
9. Oregon
10. Utah

"People were getting shot with .22s and getting up," he explains. "So we started buying .357s. Thought that was cool. Then we noticed we were running out of bullets too fast, started buying two clips, then extension clips, then AR-15s [a powerful automatic gun]."[9]

A community counselor in Detroit agrees. "That's just trivial nonsense [that starts the violence], but it results in death. Don't believe me? In Chicago last summer a gang war broke out in one of the projects, and over three days thirteen people were killed. The reason? Somebody was going out with a girl someone else wanted to go out with!"[10]

Choosing a Gang

The many differences between gangs make generalization difficult. For instance, although more than 90 percent of gang members are boys, there are some all-girl gangs, as well as some gangs that include both boy and girl members.

One chooses a particular gang for various reasons. Often, says one former gang member, the choice is made for you, simply by circumstance. "I didn't have nothing to say about it," says one teenager. "My neighborhood is all Crips. Nobody's tolerating no Blood or no other set walking around here. If I decide I want to be one of them guys, I might as well slit my wrists, I'll be dead soon anyway. If I'd been born east of the Texaco over there on Fifteenth Street, it'd be a different story, I guess."[11]

Another determining factor is who one's friends are. Many gang members are recruited by friends, in a purely social context. Tajan, a Gangster Disciple, came home from an extended stay in another city and found that most of his close friends had joined that gang. "I'd be just kicking with my friends," he explains,

> and it seemed like they were all of a sudden into gang stuff. They gave me some papers [about the Gangster Disciples] to read. Said they wanted to know what I

Tajan, a Gangster Disciple, joined a gang after he discovered that many of his friends had joined. He says, "I'd be just kicking with my friends, and it seemed like they were all of a sudden into gang stuff."

thought about it. I mean, they weren't making me do anything. They said, "We're not asking you; this should be on you, not a forced thing."[12]

Another motivation for joining a particular gang may be tradition. Many gangsters proudly declare themselves third- or fourth-generation. A young gangster remembers that when she was young, her cousins and uncles were all Vice Lords: "I knew about . . . being in a gang, because they were, too. . . . All of the older cousins would be there . . . and I'd watch them throwing their signs around and see them wearing their colors. . . . They'd talk to us sometimes, especially when we got to the age where we were wanting to be in the gang too."[13]

"Down with the Gang"

Many fraternities and sororities have initiations, tests or rituals that a pledge must pass or endure to become a member.

Prospective gang members, too, must pass tests to prove their loyalty. As one former gang member says, "You got to show you are down with the gang, that anything the brothers are going to do, you are right there. They don't want you if you be nervous about the cops or other gangsters. You got to show you are down, that's it."[14]

Such tests usually involve doing something illegal, such as stealing something valuable from a store, or violent, such as fighting or shooting at a rival gang member. Some gang initiations have even involved gunning down an innocent passerby, to show that the new member will do anything asked of him. A young gangster originally from Chicago recalls that his cousin was told to shoot at a lady with a shopping bag, "just to see what kind of shot he was."[15]

Frequently, new members are "jumped-in," or tested, by fighting several gang members at once for a set amount of time. If he lasts the time period without giving up, he is automatically part of the gang. As one LA gang member recalls, "Two minutes, all the time you fight back anyway you want. If you fall down, it gets longer than two minutes. So you try not to fall. What I did was I fought against the wall. I fought six guys."[16]

The jumping-in is only the beginning of gang violence. "The life," as gangsters often refer to their activities, is usually filled with stealing, selling drugs, and endless retaliation against rival gangs. For too many gang members, "the life" ends early—either with arrest and imprisonment or a senseless death in a drive-by or other shooting.

Father Greg Boyle works with gang members in a troubled section of Los Angeles. He describes the anger he feels saying funeral masses for so many teenage boys from his parish, and how little effect such events have on other gang members:

> I've buried twenty-six kids. At all the funerals, I corner a kid who's out in the parking lot by himself crying and smoking a cigarette. Thinking maybe he'll be vulnerable to hear something for the first time, I put my

arm around him and say, "You know, *mijo* [son], I never want to see you lying in a casket at sixteen." What's eerie to me is these guys always say the same one or two things: "Why not," or "You gotta die sometime." Both are indicators of a very deep and pressing despair.[17]

Difficult Questions

No one disagrees that the violence associated with gangs or drug dealing is bad for neighborhoods. However, there is a great deal of disagreement over the nature of gangs and their activities. Greenhaven's *Gangs: Opposing Viewpoints Digests* contains essays summarizing some of the controversial issues about gangs today.

For instance, although a great deal is written about the negative aspects of gangs, experts disagree about the seriousness of the problem. Some feel that gang activity is inherently violent and that gangs are a serious threat to Americans today. Others say that the media—especially movies and television—exaggerate the extent to which gangs are a threat.

The factors in young people's lives that encourage gang behavior are uncertain, too. Do people join gangs to become wealthy? To seek a caring, loving environment missing in their real family? Or to gain a measure of respect and self-worth absent in other aspects of their lives?

Finally, there is disagreement over society's proper response to street gangs. Is the answer tougher laws and stricter punishments or youth-friendly programs in gangs' communities? Can school programs properly address the gang problem? Should gangs even be treated as a problem that needs to be solved? Some experts say that the positive aspects of gang membership completely outweigh the negatives, and that society should not fix what isn't broken. The essays that follow will provide a context for discussing gangs, their activities, and society's response.

1. *Juvenile Justice Bulletin* (1991), quoted in Karen Osman, *Gangs*. San Diego: Lucent Books, 1992, pp. 9–10.

2. Quoted in Malcolm W. Klein, *The American Street Gang: Its Nature, Prevalence, and Control*. New York: Oxford University Press, 1995, p. 7.

3. James Haskins, *Street Gangs: Yesterday and Today*. New York: Hastings House, 1974, p. 31.

4. Osman, *Gangs*, p. 17.

5. Haskins, *Street Gangs*, pp. 26, 29.

6. Quoted in Irving A. Spergel, *The Youth Gang Problem: A Community Approach*. New York: Oxford University Press, 1995, p. 7.

7. Spergel, *The Youth Gang Problem*, p. 8.

8. Quoted in Gail B. Stewart, *Gangs*. San Diego: Lucent Books, 1997, p. 9.

9. Quoted in Lewis Cole, "Hyper Violence," *Rolling Stone*, December 1, 1994, p. 110.

10. Quoted in Stewart, *Gangs*, p. 10.

11. Personal interview of Brey (last name unknown), a Crip from Oakland, California, March 16, 1997.

12. Quoted in Stewart, *Gangs*, p. 20.

13. Quoted in Stewart, *Gangs*, p. 54.

14. Personal interview of Cesar, May 16, 1996.

15. Personal interview of Cesar, May 16, 1996.

16. Quoted in Osman, *Gangs*, p. 42.

17. Greg Boyle, interviewed by Sharon R. Bard, "Gang Life," *Creation Spirituality*, Spring 1994, p. 21.

CHAPTER 1

How Serious a Problem Are Gangs in the United States?

*"Gangs are largely made up of scary, vicious people. . . .
There may be other 'perks' of gang life, but to the average
'good kids' who are gangbanging, shooting and killing are
the names of the game."*

Savagery and Violence Are Inherent in Gang Life

There's a school of thought these days—especially in the sociology and psychology communities—that the gang violence we all hear about on the nightly news is a fabrication. What gangs are *really* about, we are told, is providing a secure family setting for basically good kids who lack that security, or surviving poor living conditions, or even making money. Sure, they admit, there is some violence, but the amount is overblown. It certainly is not enough to warrant all the bad publicity these "basically good kids" are getting.

I don't know what planet these sociologists and psychologists hail from, but it isn't the same one I'm living on. On my planet, gangs are largely made up of scary, vicious people, obsessed with violence and the power that goes with it. One can hardly pick up a newspaper anymore without seeing that someone has fallen victim to a gangster's gun. There may be other "perks" of gang life, but to the average "good kids" who are gangbanging, shooting and killing are the names of the game.

It isn't as though anyone living "the life," as gangbangers fondly refer to their chosen path, really starts out wanting to get shot. A twelve-year-old Richmond, California, boy named Rafael was adamant about that. "I don't want to be part of a gang," he said in an interview with *Rolling Stone* magazine's Lewis Cole. "I don't want to end up dead." However, in an illogical turn about, Rafael admits that killing others *is* one of the things that tempts him to rethink his position.

> People ask me to join, I think about it, think about the fun things they do—driving cars, smoking weed, killing people, getting drunk. I want all kinds of things. A car, a motorcycle, a moped. I want a gun, too. A MAK-90. It's an automatic. Has a clip about as long as this table. It holds 500 bullets. I like a bullet with a hollow point, so if you shoot someone, it will ricochet around in them, off all the bones. Because, if you shoot someone, why not kill them?[1]

Once a youngster joins the Crips, the Insane Vice Lords, the Bloods, or any gang in the mean streets, the violent nature of his new life becomes evident, for he himself is the first victim. The ceremony of induction is violent to the new recruit. Called "jumping-in," the process requires that the inductee spend an agreed-upon number of minutes with several of his new brethren, whose job it is to beat him bloody. Even for the growing number of girls joining gangs, the initiation is violent—although girls are given the choice of gang rape by male members (called "rolling-in") or jumping-in. One girl from the Vice Lords recalls her painful ritual:

> I chose fighting [my way into the gang]. I wasn't about to do that other thing! I figured, when you come right down to it, with all the diseases and everything, I'd be a lot safer fighting against five gang members.... Hey most of those five were cousins, and they weren't going easy at all on me. I mean, maybe *they* thought they were being kind, but it hurt a lot. I got hit hard, a couple of times in the back of the head."[2]

Once he or she is an official member of the gang, the violence turns outward—toward other gang members, girlfriends, or family members of other youths who have angered the gang in some way. A Vice Lord named Albert McGee, now serving time at the Mississippi State Penitentiary for drug possession and murder, recalls with some fondness the first time he killed a rival gang member:

> I was 15 or 16 at the time; it was more of an act to prove myself than anything he did to me or any of my brothers. I stole a car and told myself that the first person I saw who's convenient I was gonna kill. After driving around some, there was this guy I saw going to his car. I just pulled up beside him and asked the

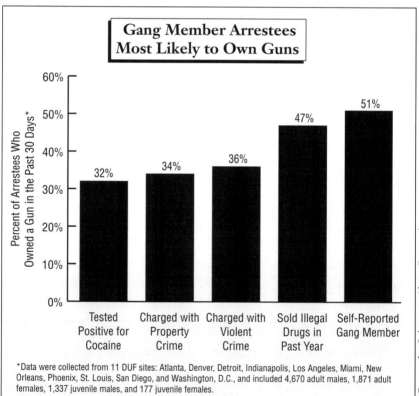

Gang Member Arrestees Most Likely to Own Guns

*Percent of Arrestees Who Owned a Gun in the Past 30 Days**

- Tested Positive for Cocaine: 32%
- Charged with Property Crime: 34%
- Charged with Violent Crime: 36%
- Sold Illegal Drugs in Past Year: 47%
- Self-Reported Gang Member: 51%

*Data were collected from 11 DUF sites: Atlanta, Denver, Detroit, Indianapolis, Los Angeles, Miami, New Orleans, Phoenix, St. Louis, San Diego, and Washington, D.C., and included 4,670 adult males, 1,871 adult females, 1,337 juvenile males, and 177 juvenile females.

NOTE: The findings above may be partially accounted for by arrestees' willingness to report deviant behaviors. Arrestees who report selling drugs or being a gang member may be more likely to admit to owning a gun.

Source: Center for Substance Abuse Research

time. Then I shot him in the face with a .357 five times—being a Vice Lord, I ride under the five-pointed star. After I shot him, I got out of my car and kicked him to make sure he was dead, which he was. Then I started dancing around and laughing, having a good ol' time. That was my first time, but not my last.[3]

Sometimes the target of gang violence isn't the gang member himself, but a member of his family. One youth remembers not being able to find the rival he was gunning for, so instead he shot and killed the rival's nine-year-old brother as the boy was playing on swings at the park. Another gang member recalls shooting a rival's mother in both knees, "just to see how loud she could scream, especially since she thought I was going to kill her for sure."[4]

Nothing, however, signifies "gang" quite so vividly as the drive-by—the sudden terror of a carload of heavily armed youths with bandannas around their heads shooting at large groups of people. By their own admission, most of them have terrible aim—"If we hit 'em, we hit 'em," said one East Los Angeles gang member. "If we don't, we don't. . . . To tell you the truth, we don't know how to shoot."[5]

Making the Rabbits Scatter

So what we have on our streets are cars filled with violent people with automatic weapons, who have no ability to aim. Screech around a corner, point, and watch the rabbits scatter, they say proudly. The "rabbits," of course are the newest group of victims of gang violence—those who wind up dead because they just happened to be in the line of fire. Elderly people sitting on their front porch, children out playing, even babies in infant seats, killed because of gangs and their need for violence.

Ask twenty-one-year-old Shalla Gillum about gangs and killing. She lost her four-year-old daughter, Davisha, to gang violence in 1996. The little girl was sitting in a car with her mother at a gas station in St. Paul, as one of Shalla's friends was busy putting a little air in the front tire. As they sat, chatting about whether to stop for ice cream before going home, gunfire erupted. Police said later that no one in Shalla's car was a target; it was almost certainly directed at a car on the other side of the service station, most likely a gang-related attack.

When the gunfire stopped, it was four-year-old Davisha, not a gang member, lying in a ball on the floor of the car, shot through the head. Her mother felt there was a sad irony in the situation. "I'm not in a gang, and hardly ever go too far away from home," she said. "I just don't like being with a whole lot of people."[6]

But her alliances didn't matter when the shooting started. As Shalla sobbed and cradled her daughter's blood-soaked body, what *did* matter was that another life had been lost, for no reason other than the love of violence that the gangs of America—these "basically good boys"—have a need to display to the rest of us.

1. Quoted in Lewis Cole, "Hyper Violence," *Rolling Stone*, December 1, 1994, p. 108.

2. Quoted in Gail Stewart, *Gangs*. San Diego: Lucent Books, 1997, p. 55.

3. Albert McGee, "Ridin' Under the Five-Pointed Star," *Prison Life*, March 1995, p. 50.

4. McGee, "Ridin' Under the Five-Pointed Star," p. 50.

5. Quoted in Earl Shorris, *Latinos: A Biography of the People*. New York: W.W. Norton, 1992, p. 116.

6. Quoted in Chris Gravesi, "I Just Want My Baby's Killer Found," *Minneapolis Star Tribune*, July 23, 1996, p. 11A.

"The whole issue of gangs and gang violence has been exaggerated and hyped by the media."

Gang Violence Is Overblown by the Media

They are everywhere, aren't they? Wherever one looks, whether in the heart of the city or an upscale suburban mall, there are gangs. They are recognizable to all but the most blind among us—with their colorful bandannas, the sagging pants (which defy gravity simply by staying up), the brimmed hats cocked to one side or the other. Donning the uniform are African American males and, increasingly these days, Latinos, Asians, or whites—and females. We see, too, the evidence of their presence—the mostly indecipherable graffiti adorning walls and mailboxes. And their tremendous influence is obvious by the fact that millions of grade-school kids (not even remotely part of a gang) can flash the secret hand signals for whose sanctity any self-respecting "gangsta" would be willing to die.

And if you believe everything you read, you, as millions of other Americans, are convinced that the single biggest domestic problem facing us all today is the drive-by bullet. Sent by the automatic weapon of a Crip or a Blood or a Vice Lord or a Rollin' 60, and intended for the heart of another gangster, that bullet could find your heart instead. You, an innocent bystander, minding your own business as you walk down a city street, or into the Gap, or line up for a movie with your kids some Saturday afternoon. The bullets are flying fast and furious, and we've all heard the heartbreaking tales of innocent people being killed in an instant, for no other reason than because they were in the wrong place at the wrong time.

But such worries are unfounded, and it's time the American public realized that. In fact, the whole issue of gangs and gang violence has been exaggerated and hyped by the media to the extent that we as a society are really unaware of the scope—or lack of scope—of gangs in America today.

"They're Just Little Babies"

Youth counselor Lou Williams is a twenty-nine-year-old ex-gangster from Los Angeles. Once a member of the Crips, he has seen gun battles, has even taken bullets in his hip and groin in a skirmish with a group of Bloods. "I've seen the stuff that happens with those gangs," says Williams. "And I'm very lucky, and very glad to be away from all that. I've got my college degree now, and I'm helping kids in the city who have it tough."

A member of the Los Angeles 18th Street gang hangs out in his neighborhood.

But Williams also says that he is amazed at the number of kids nowadays who claim gang membership. "It's unbelievable," he says, shaking his head in disgust. "I listen to these kids talk, you know, and it's like they've lived through the wars. According to them, they've all been jumped-in, they've done their dramas like drive-bys and things like that. It's incredible! And I try to think about if I weren't a former gangster and didn't know better—I'd think that 95 percent of black kids under fourteen were dangerous criminals."

But that isn't so, he says vehemently. "No way are these guys 'living the life,' or whatever it is they tell people," he insists. "They're just little babies. They're playing, dressing up, talking the talk, pretending to be something they're not. It's not a crime, no. But please," he says, holding up his hands, "spare me all the discussion about the danger-filled lives they lead. Man, most of these little guys wouldn't even make good wannabes back in South Central LA or the South Side of Chicago or whatever. They are just making it all up, just playing."[1]

Glamorizing "the Life"

If that's the case, then one would ask, Why? Why would young people want to look like criminals, why would they go so far as to pretend that they *are* criminals? The answer isn't difficult. In fact, it's evident in the movies, on TV shows, and on MTV. We have seen it in the rash of "gangsta rap" songs on the radio and the glut of gang clothing at the malls. The answer is, simply, because "gangsta" translates as "cool."

No matter what the medium, it seems that the message has been communicated that "the life" is one fraught with danger, high risks, and, if one can live long enough to enjoy it, a great deal of money from drug deals. We see "the life" in countless movies in which gangsters are portrayed as heroes persecuted by a corrupt and racist justice system. The senseless and stupid violence, quite evident in real life, is not shown in such movies. One doesn't see the victim of a shooting, sitting glassy-eyed in his own blood, as the life drains from him.

Instead, the movies concentrate on the heavy gold jewelry, the handsome gang outlaws standing on street corners, throwing their signs at one another.

The 1988 movie *Colors*, starring Robert Duvall and Sean Penn, is an example of the media shaping our perception of gangs. Real gang members from Los Angeles were used as extras in the film, and, say critics, the movie seemed to be a thinly veiled attempt to glorify gang life. Sergeant Ralph Kemp of the Albuquerque Police Department was especially critical. "While the movie was a factual portrayal of gang life," he says, "kids thought it made gang life glamorous. And the movie theaters' promoting the film by handing out blue and red bandannas [in Los Angeles movie theaters] made it worse."[2]

It's not just movies, either. Gangsta rap video performers such as Coolio, Ice-T, and Snoop Doggy Dogg glorify gang members as wealthy, well dressed, and almost always surrounded by beautiful women—a reminder that a gangster is a macho, sexy thing to be. C. DeLores Tucker, national chairwoman of the National Political Congress of Black Women, sees the danger in such videos, especially in their effect on impressionable young people. In a recent Senate subcomittee hearing on gangs in the United States, Tucker quoted a letter she'd received from a young man who had once found such videos very alluring:

> Rappers . . . made it sound so good and look so real [that] I would drink and smoke drugs just like on the video . . . thinking that was the only way I could be somebody. . . . My hood girls became ho's and b——. What's so bad is that they accepted it. You know why? Because they put themselves in the video, too, and the guns, money, cars, drugs, and men became reality.[3]

Just the Trappings

So as a result, we've got hundreds of thousands, maybe millions, of kids out there who see gang jewelry, signs, language, and dress as a way of looking cool. The vast majority have no ties at all with gangs, but it's fun to look the part. Don't buy it? Think back to your own childhood, when walking around with a basketball or football jersey of your favorite player was enough to make you feel good. It's a way of belonging, like love beads, sandals, and bell-bottom jeans were in the '70s.

The danger, of course, comes when such fads are taken so seriously that society makes judgments on people based on such trappings as cocked hats and sagging pants. In other words, we are becoming too quick to see any wrongdoing committed by a youth wearing gang-type clothing as a "gang-related crime," without looking any further. And that, say researchers, is producing some flawed thinking.

For instance, Cleveland State University researchers Douglas Clay and Frank Aquila found that many school administrators are so convinced that their schools are overrun by gangs that they are holding expensive and unnecessary seminars meant to educate the public on what they call "the skyrocket-

Critics say that movies, television, and "gangsta-rap" music have played a role in glamorizing gang life. Actors from the controversial 1988 movie Colors *pose for a publicity still.*

ing gang problem in schools today." At one such seminar, the researchers report, attendees were being briefed on how to recognize the graffiti of the Vice Lords, Gangster Disciples, Crips, Bloods, and other gangs. These signs included such items as crowns with five- and six-pointed stars, winged hearts, upside-down crosses, and pyramids. Report the researchers, "High school principals and other professionals were furiously scribbling down these gang symbols like college freshmen in a lecture hall." The most interesting part of the seminar, say Clay and Aquila, occurred when a slide of a new gang sign was shown to the group. Many gasped, recognizing it immediately as one they'd seen on the walls of their own schools. "As the seminar facilitator described the symbol's widespread distribution, attendees shook their heads ... generally expressing dismay over the sorry state of our society."[4]

Scary Graffiti

However, the foolishness of the entire discussion was made evident when a probation officer stood up and asked the facilitator of the meeting, "Is this usually painted in white on a brick wall?" The facilitator said yes, it usually was.

> The probation officer continued, "Is it usually on a wall where there are no windows?" The facilitator agreed again, and asked whether the probation officer knew anything about this new gang. The officer didn't answer, but continued his own line of questioning: "Is it usually about three feet off the ground, with white rectangles on either side of it on the ground?" At this point, one of the other task force members chimed in with, "Yeah, I've seen that, too." Undaunted, the probation officer went on, "If you go about 20 yards away from the wall, I bet you will find a white stripe painted on the ground." All eyes were riveted on the probation officer. "It's a strike zone!" he said. "It's used for wall ball. Kids throw a tennis ball against the wall, and it acts as your backstop."[5]

What this shows, of course, is that our society has to take a collective deep breath and calm down. The world as we know it is *not* going to hell in a handbasket because of the huge numbers of gang recruits among our young people. Does this mean there isn't a gang problem? Of course not—there are very real, very frightening problems with gangs in our cities today. To deny that would be impossible.

But please, as we look at the clothes and jewelry the kids are wearing, as we watch the videos they watch, and hear the music they hear, and listen to the gang "lit being spit," let's try to keep it all in perspective. Clothes, music, and words don't make a gangster, any more than a Bulls jersey with a number 23 on it would make me Michael Jordan.

1. Personal interview of Lou Williams, January 25, 1996.

2. Quoted in Sandra Gardner, *Street Gangs in America*. New York: Franklin Watts, 1992, p. 64.

3. Testimony before the U.S. Senate Judiciary Committee's Subcommittee on Juvenile Justice, February 23, 1994.

4. Douglas A. Clay and Frank D. Aquila, "'Spittin' the Lit'—Fact or Fad? Gangs in America's Schools," *Phi Delta Kappan*, September 1994, p. 66.

5. Clay and Aquila, "'Spittin' the Lit,'" pp. 66–67.

"Gangs . . . have insinuated themselves into places Americans have always held sacrosanct. . . . One of these off-limits institutions is the U.S. military."

Gangs Are Active in Business and the Military

Gang members, we all think, hang in certain areas. One expects a bunch of them in bandannas and LA Raiders hats, throwing their secret hand signals at one another in a city park, at a shopping center, or hanging around on the corner by the bus stop. If I am looking for a gangbanger, I would seek these places out first, and would probably be successful.

On the other hand, if I want to be certain of avoiding contact with gang members, I might instead frequent an expensive restaurant, the symphony or ballet, or my tax accountant's office.

However, new evidence suggests that the whereabouts of the homeboys and the homegirls is no longer such a sure thing. Gangs, it seems, have insinuated themselves into places Americans have always held sacrosanct, and they're doing it right in front of our noses.

Gangstas in the Ranks

One of these off-limits institutions is the U.S. military. A 1995 *Newsweek* investigation revealed significant gang activity in all four branches of the armed services and at more than fifty major military bases around the country. What's more, the gang problem appears to be serious enough that the military has been quietly taking steps to eradicate gang activity while publicly denying that it exists.

It is not difficult to see why owning up to gangbangers in uniform would be painful for an institution built on discipline and control. After all, these are the folks that foster the image of spit-shined shoes and of bedsheets so tight one can bounce a quarter on them! Having their recruits "chilling" at the PX while dealing crack would definitely tarnish that image. But while the armed services may be proud, they are not stupid. Allowing gangs and the violence that accompanies them to run unchecked would certainly undermine them, and they know it.

Newsweek reports that the navy's Criminal Investigative Service has developed a computerized system to report and track incidents that appear to be gang related. In addition, the army and air force have issued training manuals to help their investigators recognize gang activity. These manuals include descriptions of gang hand signs and gang "colors" as well as lists of gangster slang. Warns the air force manual:

> The influence of gangs on the USAF appears to be growing and the frequency of gang violence related to the USAF will likely increase. There is no such thing as a "wannabe." If a person wants to be a gang member, acts like a gang member, and dresses like a gang member, *he is a gang member and is just as dangerous.*[1]

Frightening Capabilities

Compared with civilian life on the streets, of course, the gangstas in uniform do not make up a sizable group. But the very fact that gangs as established and dangerous as the Crips, the Bloods, and the Gangster Disciples—not to mention "sets," or smaller groups, of these gangs—are operating on military bases is cause for alarm. As of the middle of 1995, their crimes have included at least ten homicides as well as plenty of drug trafficking, assaults, and robberies. "Army enlisted men have been photographed flashing gang signs in the middle of the Persian Gulf War," reports Gregory Vistica of *Newsweek*, "[and] there are even reports that gangs stake out 'turf' on aircraft carriers at sea."[2]

The U.S. Justice Department, too, has recognized the potential for danger in this situation. In November 1994, it convened a street gang symposium, prompted by Attorney General Janet Reno, and produced a frightening report. Among other things, the report stated that

> some gangs have access to highly sophisticated personal weapons such as grenades, machine guns, rocket launchers, and military explosives. Some street gang members who are or have been in the military are teaching other gang members concerning the use of tactics. . . . With arms, weapons proficiency and tactics, some street gangs now have the ability to effectively engage in terrorist activities within the United States."[3]

Inside Legitimate Business, Too

Though it does not involve access to an arsenal, the infestation of legitimate American businesses by gang members is nonetheless dangerous. Throughout the country, gangsters are getting jobs in successful businesses, and then robbing them blind. Such sabotage goes on from warehouses to front offices, say experts. "A new wave of gangsters who boast college degrees participate in a global crime empire and actually hold jobs in the warehouses [and] offices . . . of America," warns Van Ella, president of a Chicago firm that conducts applicant screenings for large corporations. "It's beyond the scope that most people could ever imagine."[4]

How do they do it? A recent study by the University of Chicago found that gang members are increasingly adopting a middle-class appearance—losing the baggy pants and over-size sweatshirts—while duplicating techniques used by organized crime. Some street gangs subsidize college for some of their brightest young men and women, hoping that a degree in finance or business can gain them an advantage in the corporate world. According to the study, some Asian and South American gangs are using advanced computer science education to steal electronics and high-tech components.

The reasons gangbangers can get away with this kind of thing can be blamed on the new '90s workplace, say experts. Frustrated executives like Frank Johns of Pinkerton Security say it is far easier to penetrate a company than it was twenty-five years ago. "Despite a greater emphasis on screening applicants and providing security," he explains, "there's greater opportunity for abuse."[5] These opportunities are no secret to businesses, for they simply reflect the changes in society as a whole: Employees are less loyal to employers, turnover is higher, and employers place greater emphasis on outsourcing, i.e., jobbing out work to small companies which used to be done in-house.

Gangs plant members in the shipping or dispatching departments of a company and gain access as temporary workers. From these positions it is possible to reroute expensive shipments or simply gain information. Recently a Chicago pharmaceutical firm found that because it had unknowingly hired gang members in mail delivery and computer repair, more than $1 million a year in computer parts were disappearing and then being sold to computer stores.

Skirting the Law

Part of the appeal of gang activity in business is that it is far less susceptible to arrest or suspicion. Unlike crack or cocaine, no law exists against having microchips or other computer parts in one's possession. Microchips weigh less than an ounce each, and one SIMM strip (single in-line memory module) carrying several chips can bring in $400 or more, so a legitimate-looking gangster could make thousands by selling a single briefcase-full to a computer store. In fact, say police, a legitimate computer store can innocently buy from a gangster posing as a computer distributor. "A police officer who stops someone with a briefcase full of SIMMs can't assume they're illegal," says one San Jose police investigator. "There are many legitimate people in the business who carry chips around, just the way diamond brokers in New York City carry around their goods."[6]

The problem of gangs in the workplace or the military is not likely to disappear anytime soon. After all, the police and others who work with gangs can do little more to keep up with the gang members that are *visible*. The crime rate and violent activity among those gangsters is too much for society to handle. So what chance do we have against the gangsters whose colors and signs are hidden behind army uniforms and pinstripe suits?

1. Quoted in Gregory Vistica, "'Gangstas' in the Ranks," *Newsweek*, July 24, 1995, p. 47.

2. Vistica, "'Gangstas' in the Ranks," p. 48.

3. Quoted in Vistica, "'Gangstas' in the Ranks," p. 48.

4. Quoted in Samuel Greengard, "Have Gangs Invaded Your Workplace?" *Personnel Journal*, February 1996, p. 46.

5. Quoted in Greengard, "Have Gangs Invaded Your Workplace?" p. 48.

6. Quoted in Greengard, "Have Gangs Invaded Your Workplace?" p. 49.

"[Gang activity] can happen uptown, downtown, out where there's nothing but cow pastures and feed stores. . . . [T]he reasons kids get together and do this stuff are not reasons monopolized by black or Hispanic kids from the projects."

Gangs Are Not Confined to Urban Areas

Anyone who thinks "gang" translates automatically into "inner-city hoodlums" hasn't been listening for a few years. Although the stereotype might have been valid back in the '60s when it was the Sharks versus the Jets in Leonard Bernstein's *West Side Story*, the gangbangers of today are literally everywhere. The "hoods" they occupy no longer comprise a few motley blocks or a debris-littered playground. Instead, they now occupy the "bad" neighborhoods and housing projects of American cities, the fashionable streets of the urban elite, the little farm towns, and the sprawling suburbs.

From the "Butter Condos" to the Streets

One of the most recent developments in the swanky sections of New York City is the involvement of very wealthy white kids in gang activity. Although their fashionable neighborhoods may border the poorest sections of the city, financially the new gangs are light-years away. Wearing $450 ski jackets, Tommy Hilfiger sweaters, and pricey spray-painted Nintendo

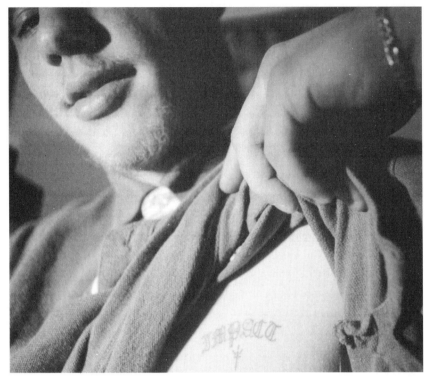

New members receive tattoos after passing the final step in their initiation into the gang. A new member of the Impact gang shows off his tattoo: a cross with three extra points, which the members say signify friendship, loyalty, and respect.

hightop sneakers, these are the sons and daughters of Wall Street millionaires, famous journalists, and TV and movie stars. They cruise around in bullet-proof Mercedes limousines giving orders to African American drivers the age of their grandfathers, selling and making deliveries of drugs to their "custies," or customers.

Their names sound a lot like those of the inner-city gangs—Double-Nine Crew (DNC), Who's King Now (WKN), and Homies for Life (HFL). One of the key differences, however, is that these gangs are providing drugs to a market of other wealthy kids, servicing the best prep schools in New York.

Their activities resemble the inner-city gangs', too. Many sell marijuana and cocaine to their wealthy customers in what the gangs call the "butter condos," the highest-priced apartments in the city, where many also live. Others steal credit cards, scam classmates out of expensive electronic equipment, or simply "bomb"—write graffiti advertising their gang. Some of these gangs commit robbery and assault.

To many criminologists and social workers who have studied gangs over the years, the existence of wealthy urban gangs is baffling. After all, these kids hardly need the money, and they're certainly not bonding together for safety in their own neighborhoods, as inner-city gangs do.

Many of the kids claim that being in a crew, or small gang, is a surefire way to gain status among their wealthy teenage friends. "It's what makes you popular," explains one eighteen-year-old, a senior at a prestigious Manhattan private school. "Ohmigod," shrieks one to a New York reporter who spent time interviewing them. "You know how lucky you are to *be* with us? Some kids would *pay*." [1]

Some brag excitedly of having "slaves"—kids so besotted by gang allure that they would do anything for the privilege of hanging with them for a while. Such "slaves" get cash or turn over personal credit cards (with balances always paid by their parents) for the gangs' enjoyment. But perhaps the most often listed reason for their gang's existence is that it provides them amusement. "We know a lot of kids who have to do what they do," one crew member says. "We do it 'cause it's fun," [2] another confesses happily.

Gangbanging in the Heartland

Gang experts admit that they would be hard pressed to name a place where gangs *don't* exist. Gangs exist even in Lunada Bay, an ultrawealthy section of southern California, where a group called the Bad Boys assault and intimidate others who would dare surf in what they consider their own turf.

Gangs have also spread to areas where naiveté is legendary, the small towns of the Midwest. Experts say gangs exist in even the smallest and most pastoral of places. Malcolm Klein of the University of Southern California finds that only one hundred American cities and towns reported gang activity in 1970, compared with almost eight hundred now. Another national survey of small-town police chiefs found that 47 percent considered drugs in their towns—often supplied by gang members—an "extremely serious" or "quite serious" problem. A case in point is Sandy Level, Virginia.

With a population of only eight hundred, it would seem impossible for Sandy Level to have a crime problem, but it does—in a big way. Crack, and the youths who sell it, has turned the little town of two square miles into a beehive of gang activity. Located in an isolated corner of the county near the North Carolina state line, Sandy Level is an unfortunately ideal setting for drug dealers. County police, who number only six at any one time, can hardly cover the area when drug dealers use high-tech scanners to monitor their whereabouts.

The twenty-five or so gang members who sell the drugs literally have the town under siege, say residents, and there doesn't seem to be anything anyone can do about it. "Parents stop their children from playing in their yards or biking down the street," writes one reporter. "Sandy Level's juvenile drug dealers act like masters of the universe, but their stature is measured by what's in their pockets—usually $500 and a gun. . . . They deal from houses and trailers overflowing with drugs, food, and booze."[3]

One resident says he has lived amid violence and drugs in New York, but that Sandy Level is worse. "People in New York shoot in the air," he says. "People here shoot at you. They's cold killers, and the oldest one might be 19. . . . They murder for a bag of potato chips, and they don't get caught."[4]

Money to Be Made

Where there is money to be made, it seems, gangs and drugs—usually synonymous these days—cannot be far behind. Sometimes the culprits are youths who move with their families from larger cities, bringing drugs and related crime with them. But more and more often, it appears that gangs from the larger cities are targeting wealthy suburbs and setting up franchises there for the drug trade.

The Gangster Disciples, for example, already have a systematic grip on Chicago and its surrounding suburbs. The Illinois State Police reports that "Chicago-based gang members have been stopped, searched, or pulled over for one reason or another in virtually every county of the state."[5] The same gang, the FBI recently reported, organized a crack ring in the sleepy town of Springfield, Missouri, hundreds of miles from Chicago, and were making sales of over $50,000 a month there.

The problem appears to be as intractable in the affluent segments of cities, suburbs, and small towns as it is in the inner city. Easy money is a powerful incentive, and criminals are not going to be persuaded to stop without a fight. As one gang counselor from a Midwest high school says:

> It doesn't seem to matter where the stuff happens. It can happen uptown, downtown, out where there's nothing but cow pastures and feed stores. The reasons are common. Kids aren't supervised; divorce is more common than two-parent homes. Loneliness, isolation, and a need to belong—those are the keys. We've got to get the message out there that these things, the reasons kids get together and do this stuff, are not reasons monopolized by black or Hispanic kids from the projects. These reasons are everywhere."[6]

1. Quoted in Nancy Jo Sales, "Teenage Gangland," *New York*, December 16, 1996, p. 32.

2. Quoted in Sales, "Teenage Gangland," p. 33.

3. Victoria Pope, "Crack Invades a Small Town," *U.S. News & World Report*, April 22, 1996, p. 42.

4. Quoted in Pope, "Crack Invades a Small Town," p. 42.

5. Quoted in "Gangs in the Heartland," *Economist*, May 25, 1996, p. 29.

6. Personal interview of youth counselor Ray Johnson, June 2, 1997.

CHAPTER 2

What Factors Encourage Gang Behavior?

"For many of these kids, the gang is family. . . . [Gangs] provide security, love, acceptance, and safety in a world that offers none of those things."

Young People Join Gangs to Find a Family

Anyone who has ever taken an introductory course in psychology has heard of Harry Harlow and his experiments with monkeys. During the 1960s, in Madison, Wisconsin, Harlow proved that babies raised without warmth and affection become dysfunctional adults, incapable of loving or showing affection to their own young. Harlow fashioned two "mother" monkeys as substitute parents for baby monkeys: One always had a supply of food, but was made of wire, and the other was soft and cuddly, yet offered nothing more than a good snuggle. The baby monkeys preferred the cuddly mother, even though it offered no food.

It should come as no surprise that many young people who join gangs have no functional family. This lack of love and trust in their own homes is what makes "the life" so downright appealing. Research supports this conclusion. Juvenile officers report that about 70 percent of kids arrested for gang or other violent activity live with a single parent who struggles to support children.

Two-Parent Households the Exception

Consider the rapidly changing picture of America's poorest families, whether they are white, African American, or Latino.

In the low-income neighborhoods of American cities, where the most gang activity takes place, the number of kids from single-parent homes (usually headed by a mother) is skyrocketing, especially among African Americans. In 1960, almost 67 percent of African American kids had two-parent homes; today the number is hovering at just 32 percent. The trend is the same for poor white and Latino kids.

What's wrong with a mother (or sometimes grandmother) raising kids alone? Nothing, necessarily, except that it's much harder for one parent to do the work of two. One parent usually means half the income, half the amount of attention paid to children, half the discipline and love, half the patience when times are stressful.

An Easy Step to Dysfunctional

In a great many families of gang members, the mother is too busy working to pay adequate attention to the comings and goings of her children; she often works long hours, making it impossible for her to be home when her children are. It is easy for a child, therefore, to find trouble when he spends long hours on his own. Youth counselor Joe Marshall explains the reaction of that child in his book about Los Angeles gangs, *Street Soldier:*

> So here sits the homie with a daddy he never sees, hardly knows, and deeply resents. Hell, Daddy's probably in prison anyway. Mom's home being both Mom and Dad, but too often now she's strung out herself, buried too deep in her own problems to worry about fixing snacks or checking the bookbag when her son gets home from school.[1]

The picture is worse, of course, when there is no job, and parental despair is coupled with drug or alcohol addiction, neglect, or child abuse. Celeste Fremon, who interviewed a Los Angeles priest who devotes himself to working with gang kids, was appalled at the lack of functional families among gang members:

> Pick three, any three of the gang members that hover around Boyle's door, and delve into their family dynamics and the story will disturb your sleep. There is Bandito, whose father died two years ago of a heroin overdose. There is Smiley, whose father is continually drunk and abusive. There is Gato, whose basehead [crack addict] mother sold his only warm jacket to buy a hit.[2]

Such a sad state of affairs pains older residents of poor neighborhoods, for although gangs and crime certainly existed a generation ago, they were not nearly so prevalent. In those days many parents looked out for other people's kids, too. "With me, I always shared," explains one older resident. "It didn't matter if your mom smoked dope or was an alcoholic; if you were a kid and came to my house, you ate. That's the way I was raised. Now I'm afraid to come out my door. You never know when these kids are gonna act up because they have no heart, morals, respect."[3]

And even when two parents are in the home, too often what is learned is not "heart, morals, respect," but violence and disrespect. One gangbanger's father casually mentioned a fight he'd had with his mother-in-law:

> She come in the house one time. I grabbed her behind the neck and get my shotgun—I love shot-guns—and I can jack up and shoot with one finger, and I put it in her mouth and tell her, "I told you no more hollering and screaming." She just cried.[4]

In addition to being deprived of strong family love and support, many gang members lack the maturity to head families of their own. To many, the idea of marrying and being responsible for rearing a child is ludicrous. One fourteen-year-old gang member says:

> I know that marriage is for suckers. . . . You ain't got to marry nobody 'cause they going to have a baby. What's a baby? If I get a b—— pregnant she can go have it or whatever else she want, 'cause the kid don't give a s——. . . . Look at me, didn't nobody care about me when I was a baby, and I came out cool, so what's the big deal?[5]

How We Have Failed

With attitudes and influences such as these, is it any wonder that a gang has more appeal for kids than their own families? "For many of these kids, the gang *is* family," says one social worker. "They provide security, love, acceptance, and safety in a world that offers none of those things." Another ex-gang member agrees:

> Gang culture is ghetto male love pushed to its limit. . . . Gangs offer kids security in a f—— environment. It's not the killing that initially draws a kid into gangs. It's the brother-like bond, because you're telling the kid, "Yo, I love you, and if anything happens to you, those mother—— are going to be dead.[6]

Brooklyn gang members show their gang sign at Coney Island. For many kids gangs take the place of their families.

But the sad fact is that, while many of the older gangsters may start out as father figures or counselors for the youngest recruits, they are not equal to the task. They have not learned to love and be loved. They have not learned patience and humor, tools necessary for guiding young people. So trust is betrayed once more, young people learn quickly that even in a gang, no unconditional love or acceptance exists. They are alone in a dark, cold place, and it is their willingness to be ruthless that allows them to survive.

Without familial bonds, without love and security, these gang members are doomed to repeat the antisocial, violent, dysfunctional behavior that they have witnessed in their homes. "Somewhere, somehow, we have failed to humanize a generation," says psychologist Grady Dale, "and we are seeing the results. The blank stare, devoid of emotion, that I see when interviewing troubled teenagers tells me that the child has never experienced warm, affirming emotional support."[7]

The future, for a society that claims to want to put an end to the gang violence and crime on the streets, is bleak unless these kids get this kind of necessary support.

1. Joseph Marshall, *Street Soldier: One Man's Struggle to Save a Generation*. New York: Delacorte, 1996, p. xxiii.

2. Quoted in Karen Osman, *Gangs*. San Diego: Lucent Books, 1992, p. 36.

3. Quoted in Lewis Cole, "Hyper Violence," *Rolling Stone*, December 1, 1994, p. 110.

4. Quoted in Cole, "Hyper Violence," p. 113.

5. Quoted in Carl S. Taylor, *Dangerous Society*. East Lansing: Michigan State University Press, 1990, p. 49.

6. Ice-T, "To Live and Die in LA," *Playboy*, February 1994, p. 139.

7. Quoted in JoAnn Bren Guernsey, *Youth Violence: An American Epidemic?* Minneapolis: Lerner, 1996, p. 19.

"When you're in a set you not only gain power, you gain rebellious power. You're not answering to anybody."

Young People Join Gangs to Gain Respect

Respect is one of the most frequently mentioned reasons gang members cite for engaging in illegal behavior, such as fighting or selling drugs. To understand a gangbanger's need for respect is not easy for people who have never lacked it. Respect on the streets in poor inner-city America is not at all the same as respect in upper- or middle-class areas.

If I am a middle-class white kid from a nice suburb, there are lots of established ways for me to earn respect. I can excel in my classes, maybe get on the honor roll. I can run for Student Council office and take votes for me as a measure of respect. I can work hard on the basketball court or the football field and hope I letter in a sport—a letter jacket is instant respect in high school. It's entirely possible that I could earn the respect and admiration of people in my community by being honest and helpful. Maybe I'm a Boy Scout, or maybe I volunteer with my church youth group to build houses for Habitat for Humanity, or help sandbag the banks of the Red River during the spring flood season. These are standard ways to gain respect, by peers and adults alike.

But it's a different world where the gangbangers—or the wannabe gangbangers—live. There, accolades in school are not an accomplishment worthy of respect, nor would Student

Council or even building houses for poor people. "What matters with the kids I hang with is pretty much two things," says Baby, a fifteen-year-old member of the Latin Kings. "It's all about paper [slang for cash] and being hard, being brave. If you got those things, man, you're a leader, you're the boss. You got all the respect out there that you need."[1]

A former gangster from Los Angeles agrees:

> The ultimate rush for any man is power. When you're in a set [a subgroup of a gang] you not only gain power, you gain rebellious power. You're not answering to anybody. Once a kid can flick this switch in his head and say, "I can do what I want to do. There are laws, but I'm gonna handle it my way," his ego is boosted. He gains identity.[2]

Routes to Respect

One way a gang member can get that identity or respect is proving himself as fearless. An activity called bailing is used by the toughest, most fearless gangbangers. Wearing gang colors while strolling through rival turf—for example, a Crip wearing his blue bandanna while walking through Blood territory—is bailing. "To anybody on the outside," explains one former Crip, "they're insane. Why would you walk down the street like a big target? Because in an aggressive environment, it's your way of saying, 'I'm not afraid of anybody.'"[3]

Having done time in prison is another way to attain the respect of others. Tito, a seventeen-year-old gangbanger, signaled his ex-con status by tattooing a teardrop on the corner of his eye. More than anything else, he claimed, that tattoo made him a man:

> The tear is going to be telling to everybody that I did time, you see. People step out of the way when they see something like that on your face. It means you down by law and they better step off. My mother when she saw it on my face says to me, "Tito, you

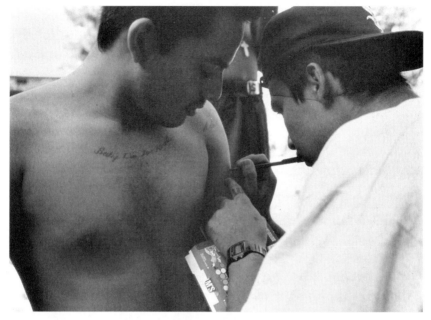

Tattoos carry many symbolic meanings including gang identity and status.

sick? What's a matter with you?" She don't see so well so she thought it was some kind of sore or something. I says, "Ma, I ain't sick, I'm a man now." She starts to crying and says, "What kind a man gonna mess up his face so no girl ever want to become his wife?" I told her, "Listen, Ma, you know what this does to girls?" They know you're bad and they all want to be with you. They know you going to protect them on the street. They know you ain't a boy. . . . It stands for something. It's like if you was wearing a football insignia or something. "I stand for this. This is me. You see this, you see me." No sissy going to be wearing one of these under his eye or he going to get challenged.[4]

Many gang initiations include shooting someone, often someone whom the assailant does not even know. One gang wannabe named Jacob remembers that he worked so hard to get a gang leader named Honcho to notice him. He made homemade weapons, knives out of wood and plastic so that

Honcho's gang could avoid the metal detectors at school with their weapons. Although Honcho was impressed by Jacob's ingenuity, he still demanded final proof of Jacob's reputation—shooting a member of a rival gang. As Jacob shrugs, "By that time, I had already worked so hard to impress Honcho that one last act—shooting someone—wasn't as hard as I expected it to be."[5]

One former gangster and heroin addict named Twace, from Brooklyn, New York, emphasizes the need for respect in his neighborhood, even if it means killing someone. "This is all because you gotta be somebody, because you gotta be down," he says. "Your name has gotta ring. And if your name don't ring, you ain't nobody."[6]

But, he says, it's not just his predominantly Puerto Rican neighborhood that demands such a reputation. "It's not just me. . . . It's every neighborhood," he insists.

> From blacks to Puerto Ricans, to white boys to Chinks to everything. There's always got to be a leader . . . and I was willing to be the leader. Sometimes my brothers, my homeboys, my friends, they would say, "Twace, you gotta chill out, 'cause one day you're gonna get killed. There's going to be a guy who maybe is crazier than you who's going to take you out.". . . I didn't care.[7]

According to gang members who have served time in prison or juvenile detention centers, a reputation for being tough or "being crazy" is critical. The top level of one pecking order behind bars is solidly based on whoever is the meanest, the most unpredictably violent.

> The people I was with, they were punks. . . . So I was on my own basically, sixty-some guys to a dorm. I had to rip a couple of people up, you know. And after that people were doing me stuff, people begging me so they can clean my clothes for a cigarette. When you're in there, you got to have the respect

you had in the street. . . . To this day [now that we're out] they see me and they don't even look at me because they're degraded, you know.[8]

Respect from Spending "Paper"

Another way that respect and status are gained is very similar to the nongang world—the proof of financial success. Among middle-class and upper-class people, a large home, a fancy foreign car, and the ability to provide an expensive college education can convey to others that one has achieved financial success. Within gang society, the same principle applies. Instead of homes and college educations, however, the tokens of success are usually lots of gold and expensive designer clothing.

One member of the Vice Lords, for example, spent over $2,500 getting gold inlays, crosses and ram's horns, on his upper front teeth. Some Crips, needing a place to use as a headquarters for their crack business, bought a house for more than $100,000 in cash. And while others might criticize the lavishness of their purchases, those who are familiar with the gang neighborhoods say that because of the abject poverty from which many of the gang members come, it is easy to see why such expensive luxuries are appealing.

One legal worker remarks, "I have one defendant [member of a gang] who's just been convicted of Murder I. He never had a bed when he was growing up. His mom was an addict, then his grandmother. They were living in a house with eleven kids, four adults, two bedrooms, no lights because they didn't pay the bills. I couldn't even find any school records on him because they moved all the time."[9]

One gang member remembers idolizing one of his friend's older brothers simply because of the way he used his money. "I can remember Jake's brother bought all of us some new Breaker jackets 'cause he used to be with our crew. We went to a steak restaurant, about fourteen of us, and he paid for everything: jackets and big steak dinners and desserts. It was def!"[10]

Girls who associate with gangsters reinforce the idea, too, that without money, a boy has no reputation, no status. One girl in a gang was asked by an interviewer whether she would ever date a boy who was not in a gang. "If a guy ain't got no crew [gang]," she says, "he probably ain't got no cash. Guys with no paper don't interest us. If you ain't got no paper, what do I need you for?"[11]

"No One Can Take It Away"

The gangbanger's constant need for gratification, for respect, for status is a frequent topic of discussion among community workers trying to make a connection, trying to get the kids out of the gang and into something more sane. Joe Marshall, a former teacher who now works with gang members in some of Los Angeles's toughest neighborhoods, says that misplaced notions of respect account for most of the gang members' mistakes on a daily basis, especially the notion of respect coming from other people:

> I have no problem with lusting for respect as long as one is after the proper kind of respect—that which, like change, comes from within. It is the materialistic pursuit of respect from other sources that warps the brothers' values. They think that the right clothes and jewelry will bring them respect from others. They think that the right car and a fat roll of bills in their pocket will do it. They think that guns and a rep and making babies will do it. They are constantly chasing respect and are baffled when they accumulate all the trappings and it still remains elusive. They don't understand that they can't *earn* respect, because if they're dependent upon someone else to give it to them, then someone else can also take it away. They don't understand that respect is something they have to give to themselves. If they do that, no one can take it away.[12]

1. Personal interview of Baby, February 1, 1996.

2. Ice-T, "To Live and Die in LA," *Playboy*, February 1994, p. 139.

3. Ice-T, "To Live and Die in LA," p. 139.

4. Quoted in Ben Sonder, *Gangs*. New York: Benchmark Books, 1996, p. 40.

5. Quoted in Debra Goldentyer, *Gangs*. Austin, TX: Steck-Vaughn, 1994, p. 46.

6. Quoted in Susan Goodwillie, ed., *Voices from the Future: Our Children Tell Us About Violence in America*. New York: Crown, 1993, p. 96.

7. Quoted in Goodwillie, *Voices from the Future*, p. 99.

8. Quoted in Goodwillie, *Voices from the Future*, pp. 100–101.

9. Quoted in Lewis Cole, "Hyper Violence," *Rolling Stone*. December 1, 1994, p. 108.

10. Quoted in Carl S. Taylor, *Dangerous Society*. East Lansing: Michigan State University Press, 1990, p. 96.

11. Quoted in Taylor, *Dangerous Society*, p. 59.

12. Joseph Marshall, *Street Soldiers: One Man's Struggle to Save a Generation*. New York: Delacorte, 1996, p. 32.

"For one wanting to get rich, but who has no education or skills to speak of, the drug business seems made to order."

Kids Join Gangs to Become Wealthy

I get weary of the argument that lives of poverty and oppression make young people turn to gang life—that because of the lack of jobs and opportunities for young people in our cities, no simple alternative exists but to sell crack and other illegal drugs. I don't dispute the poor backgrounds of many gang members, or their limited job opportunities. But I emphatically deny that the alternative to "poor" has to be "rich." Greed, not earning a living, is the carrot that makes the gang beast go. It is the promise of a life of luxury, of wanting for nothing, that lures many young people into gangs.

The Drug Business

For one wanting to get rich, but who has no education or skills to speak of, the drug business seems made to order. One has only to take a risk by holding the product, and the customers come (in droves, apparently) to you. And for poor kids with not many options other than working at some fast-food place, it's not that hard to see how in their eyes, the prospect is enticing. Many dealers admit that the money can be as intoxicating as the drugs they sell.

Until the drug business became so lucrative in the inner city, it was difficult for most kids to earn a regular income (legally, anyway). Many gang kids dabbled in petty thievery and extortion from area shopkeepers and residents, but aside from getting a job at the local fast-food joint, there wasn't much work.

"The minute cocaine changed from being the champagne of drugs for the rich people to being sold as a little rock's worth for a couple of bucks, everything changed in the neighborhood's economy," says one boy who has sold crack for eight months.

> Nobody's hardly walking around with bags of coke on them no more—it's just the rock that you can carry easy in your sock or your mouth in a little bag or something, and you're ready to go. And you don't have to travel out of your neighborhood to sell it— everyone wants a hit, right now. And they just are happy as anything to hand over their money to you, and chances are they'll be back in a little while for some more, too.[1]

How much money are we talking about here? Experts say that it's not unusual for a thirteen-year-old to make between $300 and $500 in a single evening. One boy in South Central Los Angeles boasts that he made $300,000 in one year. Crack is, they say, the number-one employer of minorities in America. And for those young people, it is an opportunity to have all those expensive things which they think can guarantee them the status and respect they desire.

One high school teacher notes that it isn't difficult to spot the kids that are selling drugs in his school. "Some of the boys I see can go three or four weeks and not repeat the same outfit," he laughs. "And we're talking really expensive designer stuff. And the jewelry is something else—lots of chains—as thick around as your middle finger. I don't even *want* to know how many weeks I'd have to work teaching to afford one of those chains!"[2]

Reuben was a young drug dealer that gang expert Joe Marshall was counseling in the San Francisco Bay area. He describes the first time he realized that his minimum wage salary was almost laughable compared with the work his cousin did:

> I was getting up every morning and going to work until one day I watched my cousin go outside and come back in the house a couple hours later with more money than I would make busting my butt for two weeks. I asked him how can I be down. We went to Palo Alto together, bought some drugs, and it took off from there. . . . [I] sold dope for about four years. I tell people I was close to being a millionaire. I would say, "Do you know what it feels like to yawn and have a hundred thousand dollars put in your face? Do you know what it feels like to do nothing and have money fall in your lap?" I used to sleep with thousands of dollars lying in the bed with me. I'd just lie there, sleeping in money. Money had to be around me. I couldn't go out of the house without at least a thousand dollars in my pocket."[3]

Although Reuben later wished he had never become involved, there are plenty of kids in the same situation today, sneering at those around them who are more than willing to work at McDonald's or another low-paying job to make honest money. In Detroit, researcher Carl S. Taylor interviewed gang members, asking them if they would be interested in working in a nearby automobile plant. The first boy, Dickie, laughed.

> Work in a plant? Are you ill? Plants be noisy, dirty, and have mugs screaming bull—— orders—and they pay ho-wages. That money ain't s—— compared to rolling. I'm going to roll until I leave here. My momma talk about how proud she is of me making doughski [money]. She used to dog me and say I wasn't s——, but now she's proud. See, when you getting paid, everybody, I mean everybody, want to get with you."[4]

Another boy, sixteen-year-old Rodney, shook his head in answer to the question about a factory job, and explained how the real money in his neighborhood was made:

> Hell, no. . . . The plant is for suckers. My cousin Darren worked at Fords and he thought it was happening. He worked all day, overtime, all the time for peanut money. Now my boy Jerome he's younger than Darren and he already got two brand new rides [cars]. He works when he wants and he's making big money. Factory money ain't no money. Jerome is rolling with the [gang name deleted]. . . . When you're rolling, life is sweet . . . you can buy anything and folks respect you. Darren told me that I could deliver pizza or work at Wendy's [laughing loudly]. Right, for three or four dollars! . . . If you get with the real fellas like Jerome did, then you get paid like big time action. . . . [Jerome's gang] drive Benzo's, 'vettes, Renegades, got big paper and all the b—— they want.[5]

As the market in the inner-city neighborhood becomes saturated, and the price of crack goes down, the entrepreneurial spirit that has driven American big business is likewise evident among the gangs. Many large gangs in Chicago and Los Angeles have taken their goods to other states, looking for larger markets and higher prices. The crack, heroin, and other drugs sold in Los Angeles, for instance, is four times as expensive out of state—a true seller's market.

Would you imagine that a kid from Los Angeles would have difficulty starting up a franchise of his crack trade somewhere in the Midwest or the Deep South? Think again, according to one former Crip:

> Everybody has a cousin in St. Louis or Cleveland and they can get their homies involved in the drug trade. A gang member flies out to see his relative, and since he has this strong identity, the kid out of state will listen. Gangsters are given respect.

Compared with these kids in Mississippi, they have it going on. A kid in Mississippi has never seen anything like it. He's dirt-ass poor, saying, "Hey, I want to be in this. I like this."

The L.A. connection will tell him, "I'm from the Rollin' 60s [a set of the Crip gang] and I have this product for you. If you have any problems or any drama out here, I'll have [other gang members] flown in from L.A. You see how we're kicking up dust in Los Angeles?" And in no time, they'll turn out about ten dudes in Mississippi. They'll dress 'em up, teach them the ropes, and now Mississippi has a gang with real members."[6]

Kids see so many good reasons to sell drugs, and so few reasons against it, that there is little incentive to get a real job, one at which they might not get filthy rich, but one they won't get killed doing. Their parents, their friends, and even their girlfriends seem to enjoy the benefits of a young person who's "rollin'."

"This boy at my school wants to get with me," laughed a girl named Angela. "He's cute, plays on the basketball team at school. I could get with him. I told him that I could get him with the [gang name deleted]. He got real ill, started acting nervous. . . . He said . . . he had a job at the gas station. I said, 'Look here, fella, how are you going to get with me and you ain't got no paper?'. . . Got no cash, got no time."[7]

Another girl bragged about her boyfriend Michael, and how much her own mother appreciates the large sums of money he makes dealing drugs. "My momma likes Michael 'cause he brings her real nice gifts," she says. "Now some boy working at Mickey Dee's [slang for McDonald's] ain't got no gift paper, you know?"[8]

1. Personal interview of Money, March 3, 1996.

2. Personal interview of tenth-grade basic math teacher in Minneapolis, March 22, 1997.

3. Quoted in Joseph Marshall, *Street Soldier: One Man's Struggle to Save a Generation*. New York: Delacorte, 1996, pp. 191–93.

4. Quoted in Carl S. Taylor, *Dangerous Society*. East Lansing: Michigan State University Press, 1990, p. 55.

5. Quoted in Taylor, *Dangerous Society*, p. 44.

6. Ice-T, "To Live and Die in LA," *Playboy*, February 1994, p.141.

7. Quoted in Taylor, *Dangerous Society*, p. 60.

8. Quoted in Taylor, *Dangerous Society*, p. 60.

CHAPTER 3

How Can Gangs Be Eliminated?

"We need a constant presence here, these kids need to see that the officers are around, and that they're watching."

Federal and Local Law Enforcement Must Get Tough on Gangs

I read about the street criminals who commit horrendous acts—drive-by shootings that kill innocent bystanders, sometimes infants in strollers, or old people sitting out on the stoop for a little fresh air in the evening. I hear about the drug sales that have turned our inner cities into war zones, and so many of our young people into worthless junkies. And then I see pictures of the criminals, and I am amazed. My God, I think, these are kids, some of them thirteen and fourteen years old, and they're using automatic weapons as skillfully as other kids that age manipulate a soccer ball or glide on rollerblades.

If these crimes were being committed by the Mafia or some other organized crime network, we would be calling for the criminals' swift arrests. We would demand that law enforcement agencies use every possible tool at their disposal to capture them, and we would demand rigorous sentencing in the courts. We, as a society, would demand that action be taken.

But these are crimes being committed by groups of young people. A great many of these criminals are too young to be treated as anything other than children processed through the juvenile justice system.

What Doesn't Work

Several things impede us from eliminating gang crime. For one thing, residents of high-crime areas constantly complain about the lack of adequate police protection. "A couple of patrols once or twice a night doesn't even come close," says one neighborhood block captain. "It's a joke—there's nothing one or two officers can accomplish like that. We need a constant presence here, these kids need to see that the officers are around, and that they're watching."[1]

Even when the police are there and can arrest criminals, there seem to be obstacles. Consider the case of two sixteen-year-old gang members who were arrested for killing an old man on a busy Detroit street in broad daylight. Although police found several witnesses to the shooting, these witnesses changed their stories before the case went to court, and the two suspects were released because of insufficient evidence. Police believe that members of the suspects' gang threatened the witnesses, intimidating them so that they were afraid to testify. It is, police say, a common problem in cases involving gangs.

In Oakland, California, for instance, police have reported several cases in which witnesses at upcoming trials for gang members have had their pagers go off, flashing what turns out to be the number of a local mortuary. "You're frustrated, you're so frustrated," says one prosecutor. "The worse the criminal is, the more likely the witnesses are to be intimidated. So you have the most heinous of criminals about to walk free because these people are so terrified."[2]

Even when young offenders are caught, tried, and convicted, their punishments are usually woefully inadequate. Consider, for instance, the case of a young gang member from Chicago who gunned down three bystanders in an attempt to kill a rival gang member. (As it turned out, he found that the boy he was aiming at was not the gang member at all.) The shooter was only fifteen, and because of his youth was given a sentence of three weeks at a young offenders' camp, which included swimming, movies, and horseback riding, followed by a seven-month stay in a junior detention facility. One former LA gangster says that any young gang offender brags that even if sent to the worst of the juvenile lockups, he could do two years, "'standing on my head.' To most of them, [juvenile] jail is no different from home. They ain't going to do nothing but kick it with the homies in jail. Everybody's there."[3]

Untie the Hands of the Justice System

How can we as a society expect criminals to change their ways if we cannot offer police the support they need to catch them? How can we expect them to fear being caught if the penalties for ending lives with violence and viciousness are no more than an inconvenience, and certainly not frightening or unpleasant enough to be a deterrent?

Some improvements have been made in individual states or communities, and these should be adopted throughout the country so that any city, town, or suburb that experiences gang crime can be protected. In California, for example, a new law has lowered the minimum age for adult charges from sixteen to fourteen. This would allow the state to try murderers, such as the three fourteen-year-old members of the Black Mob in San Diego who killed a young pizza deliveryman while attempting to steal pizzas, as adults. No more horseback riding camps. No more three-week stays at the juvenile lock-up. Real live prison—period.

One of the best new ideas is to raise the number of law enforcement officials working on gang-related activities. Local police will tell you they're woefully understaffed; to combat their problems with crack and gangs, they would have to reassign officers from other areas, where they are also needed. One plan that has been getting some positive attention lately is to use federal agents from the FBI and the Drug Enforcement Administration (DEA) to fight the growing gang problem.

Since 1992, for instance, a large group of FBI agents has joined Connecticut's state and local police to target about one hundred gang members who are responsible for most of the state's drug-related violence. In the first three years, violent crime in cities like Bridgeport was down more than 20 percent, and the results drew pleased comments from area residents and police officers. "I've gone into neighborhoods where people actually come out of their homes to say 'Thank you,'"[4] one U.S. attorney says.

Hoping to see the same results in other areas, the federal government has reassigned more of its agents—up 30 percent from 1992—and arrests are increasing. Federal officials say that the number of violent crime arrests has almost tripled within two years. FBI and DEA agents are now working in tandem with local police fighting against gangs in more than twenty cities.

Interesting Advantages

Such teamwork with the federal government is helpful in other ways besides the increase in manpower. For instance, local and state budgets cannot begin to compete with the federal government's when it comes to the number of law enforcement officials. Federal agents can be assigned in greater numbers, for longer periods of time. They have technological training and expertise that local police do not. Federal money comes in handy before the criminals go to trial, too. "Witnesses can be shielded from threats and intimidation by well-funded federal witness protection programs,"[5] says writer Gordon Witkin who has looked closely at the cooperation between federal and local police.

One advantage of cooperation between federal and local agencies is that federal prisons—an option for more young gang members if the age guidelines are lowered—are far more of a deterrent than state prisons. One Georgia drug trafficker, who is believed to have been responsible for 25 percent of Savannah's murders since 1990, was surprised when he learned he wasn't headed for a short sentence in one of the state's overcrowded prisons.

"He thought he'd do six months," remembers DEA agent Doug Driver. "He was happy as a lark until he found out we were federal [agents] and that life really means life."[6]

Maybe there are no easy answers when it comes to our country's most violent criminals. But if we keep sending the message that violent crime is something the American people will not tolerate, perhaps we can make a beginning that speaks more forcefully to the criminals in our midst.

1. Personal interview of neighborhood watch captain (name withheld), July 2, 1997.

2. Quoted in Sam Howe Verhovek, "Gang Intimidation Takes Rising Toll of Court Cases," *New York Times*, October 7, 1994, p. 16.

3. Ice-T, "To Live and Die in LA," *Playboy*, February 1994, p. 140.

4. Quoted in Gordon Witkin, "Enlisting the Feds in the War on Gangs," *U.S. News & World Report*, March 6, 1995, p. 40.

5. Witkin, "Enlisting the Feds in the War on Gangs," p. 38.

6. Quoted in Witkin, "Enlisting the Feds in the War on Gangs," p. 40.

"Gangs help to build young human beings every bit as much as families, churches, schools, and neighbors do."

Gangs Do Not Need to Be Eradicated

It has become quite fashionable in recent years to focus on youth street gangs as a major problem in this country. Gangs are being blamed for everything from the decline of urban America, to an increasing murder rate, to the skyrocketing drug use among the population. Every day there are calls for tough new laws against gang members—"law-abiding" Americans want to ban "gangsta" rap, gang colors and clothing, tagging on walls, and virtually any other reminder that gangs exist in our country today.

Those of us who dare question the new proposals to eliminate gangs and eradicate the gang culture are stared at in amazement, as though we were insane. Is eliminating youth street gangs so universal a good that there is nothing to discuss? Is it a given that gang members are, as they are regularly being called, "thugs," "animals," and "savages"?

It Might Surprise You

Take a look—a close look—at a street gang today, and what you see might surprise you. Gangs provide a lot of positive things to young people—things that they are not getting from other sources in their lives. As sociologist Daniel J. Monti writes, "Gangs help to build young human beings every bit as much as families, churches, schools, and neighbors do. . . . Gangs do not give meaning to a youngster's life, but they certainly offer ways in which youngsters can build a meaningful life for themselves and with persons their own age."[1]

A street gang provides a family for a young person who has none, or whose family is dysfunctional to the point where structure, discipline, and love are not provided. In such cases, as writer Luis Rodriguez says, the gang is "the only place where [young people] can find fellowship, respect, a place to belong. You often hear the word *love* among gang members. Sometimes the gang is the only place where they can find it."[2]

Gangster Disciple Laron Douglas feels the same way. He grew up without a father, he explains, so the gang filled that role. "I turned to my Disciple brothaz for love," he says. "They knew exactly how to treat a brotha and were always there for me, through thick and thin."[3]

But family ties are just one of the positive functions gangs serve. Gangs teach young people the difference between right and wrong, consequences for wrong behavior, and rewards for right behavior. Positive values gangs stress include loyalty, honor, bravery, and that excited spirit which seems to mark the real gang member. This spirit, this "living close to the edge" feeling, which is admittedly sometimes expressed in negative ways, is a gang member's greatest asset.

Warrior Energy

One former gang member refers to that spirit as "warrior energy," and says that it "needs to be nurtured, directed, and guided—not smothered, crushed, or corralled. [It] needs to be taken to its next highest level of development, where one matures into self-control, self-study, and self-actualization."[4] If the energy is allowed to grow and thrive, the gang member can become a strong leader, whose creativity can help society. If, on the other hand, society is so intimidated by the warrior energy in gang members it must attempt to crush it, the creative spark will be lost.

No More Dangerous than Anyone Else

The negative image many people have of gangs is false. Drug users (and sellers) and murderers are found in all walks of life. Murders happen in white affluent communities, just as they do in the poorer neighborhoods of the inner city. To blame either of these things exclusively on gangs is ludicrous.

It seems hypocritical to damn the gangs who sell crack, heroin, and other drugs, when the same standards should apply to the retailers of cigarettes, alcohol, and any other substance that can cause addiction or injury. As one fourteen-year-old gang member explains:

> Wrong? What's wrong? Look . . . [sigh] I'm doing what people want, what's wrong about giving people what they want? I ain't using [it], I just sell drugs. I'm just selling suckers what they need. If they want and I got it, why not! People get high all over the world . . . teachers, preachers, big-time business people, ball players, the whole damn world gets high.[5]

Laron Douglas says that the drug business has enabled his organization to grow and prosper, success not easily accomplished in the low-income parts of the city. "This trip is a multimillion dollar industry," he brags, "nuthin' but drug sales, 24 hours a day. We make all the money we can to uplift our glorious nation, and a lot of members are meeting their quotas." Money, not fighting and killing among the drug dealers, he says, is the key to success, and that is a lesson that the gangs are learning. "Being in the joint ain't cool for a real gangsta, a real gangsta is out on the streets making millions."[6]

No doubt many of the ways gangs make money go against what the rest of society values as moral and good. Some might attack the methods they use, the violence and fear that can be associated with gang behavior. However, it is important to look beyond the actions of a well-publicized few to the function and spirit of the gangs themselves. As one sociologist says, it is wrong for society to think it can eliminate these warriors. "[I]t is folly to destroy gangs," he writes. "One might as well try to destroy the youngster himself."[7] Society may one day be surprised to find that street gangs may be an important part of the solution to the problems plaguing America today.

1. Daniel J. Monti, *Wannabe: Gangs in Suburbs and Schools*. Cambridge, MA: Blackwell, 1994, p. 156.

2. Luis J. Rodriguez, "Rekindling the Warrior," *Utne Reader*, July/August 1994, p. 58.

3. Laron Davis, "In the Mind of a True Disciple," *Prison Life*, March 1995, p. 46.

4. Quoted in Rodriguez, "Rekindling the Warrior," p. 58.

5. Quoted in Carl S. Taylor, *Dangerous Society*. East Lansing: Michigan State University Press, 1990, pp. 45–46.

6. Davis, "In the Mind of a True Disciple," p. 46.

7. Monti, *Wannabe*, p. 156.

"The answers [to the gang problem] are often found close to home. . . . [U]ntapped resources lie there which could provide lasting solutions."

Gang Communities Themselves Can Eradicate Gang Violence

Hundreds, perhaps thousands, of studies have attempted to clarify and explain the gang problem in the United States. Sociologists, theologians, lawyers, psychologists, criminal investigators, politicians—everyone seems to have an opinion on why gangs are so prolific, how the crime associated with gangs should be handled by the police and courts, and what should become of young gang members when they are convicted of crimes. For many of those who are studying the problem, the solutions seem to be linked to expensive new programs, often at the state or federal level.

However, what many of these so-called experts do not realize is that the answers are often found close to home. Those who are intimately familiar with the youths who join gangs, the families from which they come, and the kinds of neighborhoods which seem to act as breeding grounds for gang violence know that untapped resources lie there which could provide lasting solutions. Quietly, with little or no fanfare, people in the gang communities are accomplishing amazing things.

In Their Shoes

One such answer is a program called In My Shoes, developed under the supervision of ex-gangsters in Chicago and recommended highly by the Cook County Circuit Court. In My Shoes works on the premise that gang members often feel they are invulnerable. Indeed, the posturing which is such a big part of the gang image is cool, unflappable, and arrogant. "If you can act like you are the man, then you are the man," shrugs one young member of the Latin Kings.

> It ain't so much that you gotta prove anything, it's all in your image. You gotta talk cool, and you are cool—it's the way it works. You can't act afraid, even if you are. You gotta act like you are so cool that if some dog-ass gangbanger from another set comes at you, you ain't afraid of getting popped [shot]. 'Cause if you die, then you got homies that'll be crying for you, they'll remember you.[1]

But having a cool image doesn't protect you in the real world. It's possible to get shot even if you don't act afraid. Too, there is a netherland between being cool, hanging on the corner, and being cried over at one's own funeral. And that's where people like Andre Mathews come in.

Andre is twenty-nine, a former Vice Lord who was shot in the back while playing dice. That was four or five years ago, and Andre isn't dead. He is wheelchair-bound, and will be for the rest of his life. Today, by his own admission, he is light-years away from his gangbanging days, when he was one of the most respected, hard-core members of his gang set.

Now, Andre is dealing with the more basic issues of survival, things he never knew about when he was in "the life" on the streets of Chicago. And through the In My Shoes program, he is sharing those basic survival issues with young gang offenders who are showing up to see him after they've put in an appearance in Chicago's courts.

"It's tough to think about catheterizing yourself," he tells his young visitors frankly, "or giving yourself suppositories, and dealing with the bedsores. Sometimes, I have to wear diapers."[2]

In addition to frank, graphic talk with people like Andre, the at-risk youth also gets hands-on experience living with disabilities caused from handguns in the brain-injury ward at a local hospital. There he puts on special glasses to distort his vision—to see the way many patients there do. He samples pureed beef, chicken, pears, and carrots. Nurses put gel on his lips and tongue to make even those meals tasteless and difficult to swallow. He is also shown how to operate chin-controlled wheelchairs, too.

Often the young visitors are smirking and tough as they enter the room of a disabled gang member or the hospital therapy room, but most leave with a more sober, more scared attitude, say proponents of the program. But then, that's the whole point.

"The idea is to bring [them] face-to-face with results of handgun violence, to balance the image of swaggering gang members with the reality many of them end up facing—permanent disability,"[3] remarks one who has researched the In My Shoes program. From the faces of the youth leaving Andre's room, or rinsing their mouths in an attempt to get rid of the pureed carrots, the program is working.

"You Are Like a Son to Me"

Thousands of miles away from the home of Andre Mathews and the hospitals in the gang neighborhoods of Chicago is another local solution to gang violence. This is one of the most in-your-face, confrontational ideas yet tried in the Pico/Aliso projects, the largest public housing complexes west of the Mississippi. The mile-square area is one of the poorest and most violent neighborhoods in Los Angeles. The gang violence is notorious; as one reporter writes, "If life in Los Angeles is harsh and scary, it's scariest in Pico/Aliso."[4]

But there are no police, no lawyers, no federal or state programs at work here. Instead, the mothers in the mostly Latino neighborhood take over the streets at night. One reporter described the scene one summer evening:

> Sixty-four mothers, most of them Latinas, walk in a procession into the parking lot of a tiny stucco church in the poorest part of East Los Angeles. The women shield their white candles from the evening wind and sing hymns in Spanish as they walk: "I have faith that the men will sing. I have faith that this song will be a song of universal love." In the rectory, five more mothers are completing a meeting with members of the street gang known as The Mob Crew.... A few days earlier, the mothers met with Cuatro Flats, a rival gang that claims territory two blocks east.... A week before this war claimed the lives of two boys: a 12-year-old Cuatro kid named Johnny and a 13-year-old named Joseph who was mistaken for his 16-year-old TMC brother. The deaths spurred the mothers to organize these marches and meetings with the hope of hammering out a lasting truce."[5]

The mothers are not trained in mediation or in psychology, but what they lack in technique and expertise they more than

DIVIDED WE FALL; UNITED WE STAND.

make up for in love and concern for "their boys." These *caminatas*, or walks, are powerful in their simplicity, according to their parish priest, Father Greg Boyle.

> They walk all night long on the weekends, in packs, in the projects. Their mission is dangerous and very disarming. Yet their presence makes the guys put their guns away and go inside. Part of the *caminatas'* message is, "You are not the enemy. You are our sons, but we won't allow you to kill each other." They're a force to be reckoned with.[6]

"An Enormously Complex Social Ill"

The problems gang members create are tough ones, and the gangsters themselves often make life miserable for the neighborhoods and communities where they live. Nonetheless, it is important to remember that gangs are made up of young people with a great many problems. As Father Boyle remarks, "We're dealing with an enormously complex social ill that must be addressed on many fronts such as poverty, dysfunctional family, despair, boredom, unemployment, and failure of schools."[7] How can federal or state programs—no matter how well funded—do the work of a community that is so intimately involved with a gang? How can federal employees, complete with their mega-bureaucracies, do more than the mothers of Pico/Aliso, or than the medical personnel of Chicago gang neighborhoods?

In an interview published in *Creation Spirituality*, Father Boyle recalls a sad incident when a gang member he knew was rendered brain-dead from a shot to the head. After a time in intensive care, his family decided it was best to donate his heart, kidneys, and liver.

As two nurses wheeled him to the operating room, one turned to the other and said, "Who would want this monster's heart?" The other nurse replied, "How dare you say that, you don't even know this kid. Didn't you see his girlfriend sitting by his bed for three days? Didn't you see all the friends come and kiss him and caress him and cry and say goodbye?" She understood what we're dealing with here.[8]

Like weary and frustrated parents, it is we, the individual communities, who must deal with these young people in the way that seems best to us. For we are the ones who know what we're dealing with here.

1. Personal interview of Edwin, February 14, 1996.

2. Quoted in Robert Koehler, "Scared Straighter," *Chicago*, February 1997, p. 20.

3. Quoted in Koehler, "Scared Straighter," p. 20.

4. Celeste Fremon, "Tough Love," *Utne Reader*, March/April 1996, p. 96.

5. Fremon, "Tough Love," p. 95.

6. Greg Boyle, interviewed by Sharon R. Bard, "Gang Life," *Creation Spirituality*, Spring 1994, p. 27.

7. Boyle, "Gang Life," p. 26.

8. Boyle, "Gang Life," p. 26.

"If new positive approaches to discipline are introduced to students and [school] staff, then dramatic changes will occur in gang assimilation and socialization."

Schools Can Solve the Gang Problem

Where can you find gangs today? More than in the malls, more than in the pool halls or the community centers, more than on the street corners or the basketball courts, schools see the greatest number of kids who belong to gangs. After all, most gang members are young people, individuals who by law must attend school until the age of sixteen. That the kids may not be there diligently sharpening their math skills, trying out for the school play, or preparing for their SATs doesn't matter a bit. The fact is that the gang members are there, on a pretty regular basis.

Their presence has never thrilled school staff or administrators, in whose eyes gang members represent a serious obstacle to running a safe, orderly school. In decades past, gangs were responsible for lots of graffiti, other vandalism, and an occasional fight. Today, however, the gang problems facing schools mirror those faced by the general public—shootings, assaults, and drug dealing. It is estimated that more than 3 million crimes each year, a great many of them gang related, are committed in or near the eighty-five thousand U.S. public schools. More than 270,000 guns come to school each day, some carried by children who say they are afraid of gang violence.

"My Concern Is . . . Leaving School in One Piece"

The threat of gang violence distracts and frightens many students, so that concentrating on schoolwork becomes difficult, says Principal Jetti Tisdale, whose elementary school in Bridgeport, Connecticut, borders a gang-infested housing project. Two students at the school have been shot just outside the school, in full view of their classmates. So many bullets were flying from the violence at the housing project, in fact, that custodians at the school had to install bulletproof windows. "Kids didn't want to go to class, they couldn't eat or sleep, they burst out crying," Tisdale says. "We couldn't think about teaching reading, writing, and arithmetic until we dealt with these problems."[1]

Indeed, teachers agree that they are spending far less time on academic curricula than they would like, in large part because of the changing school environment. One twenty-

one-year veteran elementary teacher from Detroit admits that her zeal for teaching has faded:

> Fear controls the kids and the teachers. These are elementary children and they know about death. Many of these students have known someone that has been victimized by violence. They see drugs, violence, every day in real life. . . . I used to look forward to teaching every day. . . . Now my concern is my car alarm and leaving school in one piece. These kids can't learn in this atmosphere. I have friends who teach junior high and high school and it's worse. I've seen kids that have serious problems over the years. But today the bad ones are different.[2]

A school counselor says that she was told by a sixteen-year-old gang member that she better watch how she talked to her or her crew might pay a visit to the counselor. A senior at an inner-city high school agrees that the schools are coping with a great deal of trouble from gangs:

> They're everywhere, big time crews . . . guys who pretend they're rolling, girls who love crews . . . it's bad. Teachers know, security knows, janitors know, principals and counselors know. . . . The guys who are rolling hard, they have bodyguards, big Benz's, sharp clothes, guns, friends, pretty girls . . . they've got it all.[3]

One More Thing for Schools to Do

There is such a strong gang presence within the halls of our schools today, in fact, that schools are the logical answer to the question, Who can best address the gang issue? No single institution comes in contact with more youth; no single institution has more caring, trained staff and personnel.

I know that there are many teachers and other staff workers who might groan, "One more thing for schools to do." It's true. In the past forty years, schools have been called on to

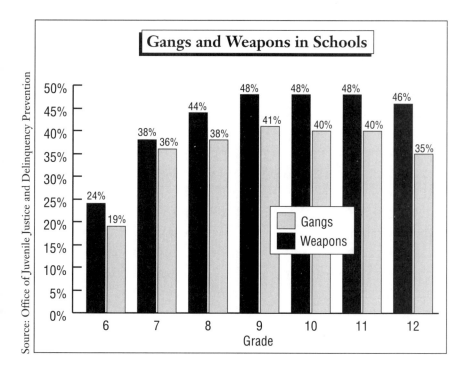

Source: Office of Juvenile Justice and Delinquency Prevention

Gangs and Weapons in Schools

solve a number of society's problems—problems that seem to baffle the rest of us. Need sex education? Leave it to the schools. How about being pioneers in racial integration? Schools, again. It seems that when we as a society want something done well, we ask the schools. And, to their credit, they've always come through. But the gang problem—that will be their toughest challenge yet.

Already, schools have led the way in initiating programs to deal with the effects of gangs. Many inner-city schools have begun "drive-by drills," training children to react quickly to bursts of gunfire outside their schools. Many other schools have built tall fences to keep older gang members from entering school playgrounds and causing problems. Hundreds of schools have metal detectors at the front doors, hoping to stanch the flow of weapons arriving each day. And back in 1993, the Los Angeles school board was the first in the nation to hire plainclothes security police armed with nightsticks to roam the hallways.

A Strategy That Will Work

These programs can help keep youngsters safe while they are in school. Of course, for any real progress to be made it is necessary to address the deeper causes of gang behavior. Some of these strategies must begin long before children are old enough to be in a gang.

Schools must adapt their curriculum to include units on nonviolence, racism, and safety if no such units exist. Teachers and administration need to make a concerted effort to reach out to parents, too. Without the strong reinforcement and support of family members, the hours a child spends in school will be wasted. "For me to spend time talking about nonviolent solutions to problems is ludicrous if the parents are slapping their child around for being late for dinner," points out one elementary teacher. "The idea is to put into practice the things we learn, and if the home is not capable of doing that, then all we're doing is spinning our wheels."[4]

Schools should also enlist more help from the larger community, recruiting positive role models who might serve as mentors for at-risk children. And schools should provide situations in which students can discuss issues that affect their lives, such as sexism, racism, poverty, and gang violence.

Assimilating Gangs

What about those youngsters who are already in gangs? Is it too late for the schools to help them? Certainly not, say educators. Principals of junior high and high schools need to make a concerted effort to reach them, for it may be the last chance gang members will have to be helped rather than arrested and jailed. But how? ask teachers, understandably fearful of confrontation with gang members.

One good method seems to be assimilation, allowing the gang to be absorbed into the school, rather than eradicating it. By welcoming each gang member, schools are validating them as people, without condoning illegal activity. One educator explains:

Former gang member Albert Juarez speaks to approximately three hundred Southern California gang members in an attempt to persuade them to return to school and to avoid turning to crime.

The radical concept that a school should accept the gangs on campus is not merely an acknowledgment, it is much more. It is the acceptance that each member is just as important as any other student and therefore should be treated like any other student. All school personnel who will be working with the gangs need to be sensitive to their peculiarities. Acceptance does not imply sanction; negative gang activity must not be tolerated. . . . Essentially, acceptance suggests that some effort will be made to change or at least to limit the negative behavior. Similarly, the basic premise of a proactive, positive, and interventive approach to gang problems is that *desired positive characteristics and behaviors increase as unwanted negative ones decrease.*[5]

Educational researchers Shirley Lal, Dhyan Lal, and Charles Achilles have found that assimilation can work by making gang members feel a valued part of the school, rather than "a problem to be solved." Interaction with gang members, for instance, is a valued part of the process of assimilation. By establishing nonthreatening communication between an authority figure such as the school principal and a gang member positive relationships can be created. In one study in the Los Angeles Unified School District in 1991, the Lals observed administrators visiting gangs at their school hangouts on a daily basis, and "when the administrator missed the meeting, the members actively sought out the administrator and inquired about his/her whereabouts. They actually expected the daily visit."[6]

Not an Easy Task

Educators admit that the process of creating a positive school climate is not an easy task. There are many small factors that individually seem unimpressive, yet when cumulatively and widely applied can be important. Most of the work is shouldered by the principal, for it is he or she who must stress the need for a positive climate at the school. Staff members and teachers will lose patience, or will not quickly accept the idea of embracing gang members into the student population, for those gang members have demonstrated only negative actions in the past.

However, it is a workable plan, and one that should be given a chance to succeed. As Lal, Lal, and Achilles write:

> [I]f the principal takes the initiative and leads the staff in an all-out effort to change student behavior, if the students are inundated with positive and proactive tactics, if students and staff are expected to behave and perform in a positive manner, and if new positive approaches to discipline are introduced to students and staff, then dramatic changes will occur in gang assimilation and socialization.[7]

1. Quoted in Thomas Toch, "When Killers Come to Class: Violence in Schools," *U.S. News & World Report*, November 8, 1993, p. 34.

2. Quoted in Carl S. Taylor, *Dangerous Society*. East Lansing: Michigan State University Press, 1990, p. 77.

3. Quoted in Taylor, *Dangerous Society*, p. 81.

4. Personal interview of a schoolteacher in St. Paul, July 24, 1997.

5. Shirley R. Lal, Dhyan Lal, and Charles M. Achilles, *Handbook on Gangs in Schools: Strategies to Reduce Gang-Related Activities*. Thousand Oaks, CA: Corwin Press, 1993, p. 57.

6. Lal, Lal, and Achilles, *Handbook on Gangs in Schools*, p. 58.

7. Lal, Lal, and Achilles, *Handbook on Gangs in Schools*, p. 61.

Appendix A

Facts About Gangs and Gang Members

—Gangs have been reported in all 50 states.

—In 1984, Los Angeles law enforcement officials estimated 450 gangs with 40,000 gang members in Los Angeles. Today, they estimate 900 gangs, with more than 100,000 members.

—Ninety-six percent of gang members are under age 25; 90 percent are between 12 and 21. The average age of a gang member is 17.

—In large cities, 1 in 5 boys is associated with a gang.

—In 1992 a nationwide survey of municipal police departments estimated that 5,000 gangs exist nationwide, with a membership of about 1 million.

—Ethnic breakdown of gangs: 54.6 African American; 32.6 Hispanic; 12.8 White, Asian.

Crimes Associated with Gang Violence

—Between 1986 and 1996, more than 3,500 people have died in gang-related violence in Los Angeles alone.

—According to researcher Allan Hoffman, studies indicate that 50 percent of juvenile crime and one-third of violent crime in urban areas is gang related.

—Four percent of high school students carried a gun in 1989.

—Approximately 7 teenagers are killed every day in youth (mostly gang) violence.

—In 1993 nearly 12 percent of students reported carrying a weapon to school at least once in the past month, according to a survey done by the Centers for Disease Control (CDC).

—The Bureau of Justice Statistics reports that 37 percent of the violent crime victimizations of children age 12 to 15 occur on school property, and much of it is gang related.

—In one survey 194 gang members were asked "Why did

you join a gang?" eighty-seven percent responded, "Because my friends are in a gang."

—In a survey of California gang members in 1991-1994, 45 percent said they made at least $1,000 a week selling drugs.

—1.7 to 2.4 million Americans use cocaine weekly.

History of U.S. Gangs

—The earliest identified American street gangs formed right after the Revolutionary War in 1783. Some of their names were the Broadway Boys, the Fly Boys, and the Long Bridge Boys. The latter two were African American gangs.

—There are three viable theories as to how the Crips gang got its name. The first is that it came from the horror movie *Tales from the Crypt*. Another theory is that the original members were crippled (they did carry walking canes) and the word was a shortened form of "crippled." The third theory explains that the gang wanted to be named after the toughest element in the world. In comic books, that would be "Kryptonite," the only mineral that could defeat Superman.

—The first girl gangs formed in the early 1950s in New York City.

APPENDIX B

Related Documents

Document 1: Street Gang Paranoia

There is no question that violent crime among young people is a growing problem in the United States. However, the media tends to exaggerate the role of gangs in juvenile crime statistics, researchers Douglas A. Clay and Frank D. Aquila contend in their article "'Spittin' the Lit'," in Phi Delta Kappan.

Once the exclusive concern of poor neighborhoods in our large cities, youth street gangs have lately inspired an almost paralyzing fear in both suburban and rural middle-class communities across the nation. . . . In this article we explore whether this perceived threat is genuine or whether it is merely the product of a growing paranoia that is being fed by those who profit from society's terrible fear of inner-city violence. . . .

The idea that gangs are linked through national organization has been cropping up frequently in the media these days. However, there is some evidence that national organization and recruitment are more mythical than real. In a 1987 study in Milwaukee, researchers interviewed that city's gang leaders. The study focused on gang organization, size, and national connections. The researchers attempted to identify the leaders of Milwaukee's gangs and conducted in-depth interviews, which were then cross-referenced with police reports in an attempt to verify statements in subsequent interviews.

The researchers asked gang members how and when their gangs began, whether they were connected with the Chicago gangs, and what sort of communication and coordination they had with other gangs. What the study showed was that, in dealing with the authorities, gang members would make up stories that police and educators wanted to hear. For example, following an assault, gang members were asked if gang affiliation was responsible for the fight. They said that it was, that they were fighting Vice Lords. After more inquiries, the gang members admitted that they didn't know whether the members of the other group were Vice Lords or not and that the fight, in fact, had started over a girl.

More research of this kind would benefit educators and criminal justice personnel alike. Too many articles on gangs start with a quote from *USA Today* rather than with one from the U.S. Justice Department or the sociology department of any university. Our guess is that the traditional male friendship cliques that have always existed are now using the language and styles of corporate gangs—not that the gangs of Chicago and Los Angeles are engaged in some national recruitment drive, targeting suburbs.

Document 2: "Spittin' the Lit": The Language of Street Gangs

One of the most fascinating—and confusing—aspects of street gangs is their unique vocabulary: a lexicon ranging from terms recycled from jazz musicians of the 1930s and 1940s to original words and phrases coined daily. In its November 1993 report Criminal Street Gangs, *the New Jersey Commission of Investigation included a list of some terms in common use. Below are several examples.*

Are you dirty?	Do you have any drugs?
Back in the day	In the past
Bad	Good
Bart Simpson	Having a new type of drug to be tried
Bo	Marijuana
C-Cypher Power	COP
Cloud	A background for a graffiti outline
DGA	An abusive insult (short for Don't get around)
Diesel	Big
Dope	Something that's cool, nice, worth having
Dropping the flag	Leaving the gang
Everything is everything	It's all right
Five-O	Police
411	Information
G ride	Stolen car
Gump	Homosexual
House nigger	Black police officer
Mellow	Close friend, as in "He's my mellow"
9 Mike	9 mm handgun
One time	Here come the cops
Rag	Gang handkerchief
Rosco	Small gun
Slash	To write over someone else's graffiti
Strapped	Carrying a gun
Twenty cents	$20 worth of cocaine
You got it like that	You got it made; you have nothing to worry about

Document 3: Violence as a Youngster's Way of Life

In an article for Rolling Stone, *Lewis Cole explores the many ways violence has become a way of life for young people in Richmond, California. Although many say that gang members honor both family ties and those with fellow gang members, Cole found that among Richmond gangs, that was not always true. At home and within one's "set," violence and distrust are affirmed on a daily basis.*

[An] 11-year-old boy treated by the Oakland pediatrician, for instance, was stabbed by his own cousin. "They were rival gang members," the doctor tells me. "His mother and the other kid's mother were sisters. Not only that, but this child and his family were having a conflict with the other family because the stabber's mother was a drug addict and would sell her food stamps and assistance money for drugs, and her kids would come to the stabber's house to eat, which she didn't like."

Set members themselves will betray you. "You can't trust your set," one gangbanger tells me, voicing a judgment the kids repeated without exception. "You can only trust individuals." And even individual loyalties disintegrate in this world. "My partner used to come to my house, pick me up, every day—we were homies," one 14-year-old says. "Then, bam! I get this gun. He's like, 'Let me see it.' I give it to him. Next day I ask him for it. So, bam! Somebody tell me that he sell my gun. I'm like, 'Man, no,' not believing. And with him I'm, 'Man, where my gun at!' He's saying no. Then we go to a party, and I see the guy they say he sold the gun to. I'm asking, 'He sell you my gun?' And he's telling me everything about the gun. I'm like, bam! 'Man, where my gun at?' 'It's at my house.' 'Go get it, go get my s—— right now.' So, bam! My partner drives off and comes back with his brother, and he say, 'What's up, nigger? I'll beat your ass.' And I say, 'What you did was wrong, nigger, we supposed to be folk.' It broke my heart because he was my partner, I was with the boy every day, and then he just did me like this because before I was trusting people."

Document 4: How to Define "Gang"

One of the most varied aspects of the gang problem is the definition of the word gang. *Below is an excerpt from an essay contained in* Schools, Violence, and Society, *edited by Allan M. Hoffman, in which Hoffman and coeditor Randal Summers show the wide range of definitions.*

Is a social group that is not involved in crime considered a gang? Law enforcement agencies typically define a gang as an organization that is based on criminal activity. [Sociologist R.C.] Huff defines a gang as "a collectivity whose members range in age from their early teens to their mid-twenties, who are frequently and deliberately involved in criminal acts, who have a group identification (typically a name and perhaps a territory or turf) for which leadership is better defined than an informal group." [Criminologist Malcolm] Klein describes a gang as "a denotable group composed primarily of values that calls forth a consistent negative response from the community such that the community comes to see them as qualitatively different from other groups." [Psychologist C.] Conly refers to gangs as "groups of youths and young adults who have engaged in a sufficient amount of antisocial activity to warrant attention by the criminal justice system."

Document 5: Making Money Selling Dope

Joe Marshall works with gang members in California and also hosts a weekly radio talk show called "Street Soldiers." In his book Marshall includes an account by a gang member named Macio in which he talks about his life making money in his gang.

I was addicted to surviving. Survival was a matter of peer pressure. I never wanted a lot of money. To me, enough money was, say, five hundred dollars at a time, enough for lunch money, clothes, going places and doing things. And I wanted a car by the time I was seventeen. And you know, we're broke all the time at home, it doesn't look like it's coming from Pops, and all your friends have new clothes, the finest girls. Women are going to the guys with the money. Your role models are the guys who are making hundreds of thousands of dollars on dope. And by that time, crack was real hot. It was the thing. And police weren't hip yet to what was going on—they weren't hip to the guys standing out on the street making money all day long. It was easy then.

The first time I went out and sold dope I made two hundred dollars in fifteen minutes working for my cousin. He bought the rocks, but since I lived in the projects . . . I was more street smart than him, so he gave them to me to sell. I ended up selling them and keeping all the money for myself because there was so much of it. I'd tell myself that I'd buy more dope and pay him back later, but I'd end up spending everything. From then on, I always kept a bag full of rocks. Whenever I needed some extra cash, I took out a couple of rocks and sold them.

Document 6: "*'Tu Eres Basura'*—You Are Garbage"
In her book Father Greg and the Homeboys, *detailing the work of Father Greg Boyle in Los Angeles, Celeste Fremon writes that at first the gangsters Boyle worked with seemed to be "an interchangeable blur," but that eventually she began to know them as individuals. When this happened, she was shocked at the bleak homes from which some of them came, as in the case of Javier Vidal and Juan Carlos Lopez—known as "Spanky" and "Cisco," respectively. It was not surprising to Fremon, after hearing about them, that many kids join gangs to feel loved and cared about.*

I learn that Spanky's father was gone long before he was born. His mother beat him with the plug end of the television cord, with the garden hose, a spiked belt—anything she could find. The beatings were so severe that she was jailed several times for child abuse. Some abusive parents are by turns affectionate and rejecting. Not this mother. In all the years of Spanky's upbringing he never received a birthday gift or a Christmas gift or even a card. "Imagine," says [Father] Greg, "not one piece of concrete evidence of caring from a parent throughout a whole childhood. One time, at my urging," he continues, "Spanky tried to reconcile with his mother. And this is what she said to the child she brought into this world: '*Tu eres basura.*' You are garbage."

In Cisco's case it was not the parents but life in the barrio that inflicted the abuse. Cisco's last memory of his alcoholic father was when he was three; his dad knocked his mother off her feet, cuffed Cisco to the floor, and snarled, "What're you lookin' at?" Cisco's mother gathered her kids and fled. However, the hotel in which she found shelter was so crime-ridden that, before he was five, Cisco had witnessed three lurid murders, virtually on his doorstep.

Cisco's mother padlocked her preschool-age children in a darkened hotel room when she went to work for the day. "She was trying to keep us safe," says Cisco. When asked if his childhood had any happy times, he thinks for a moment. "I remember this one day when my mom took us all to the park and let us run around. It was so great, you know. For once we weren't stuffed up in that little room. And we felt, I don't know, just— free!"

Document 7: "Blood Drippin' Down My Eye"

Some of the saddest—and most accurate—depictions of what it is like to live in a gang-infested world and to attend schools where gang violence is common come from the writings of children. This short essay, written by a young boy named Arnoldo, was published in "What's Happening," a newsletter for and about kids in New Jersey gang neighborhoods.

Blood Drippin' Down My Eye

Six stitches over my eye. Hit with a bat in front of Pyne Poynt Middle School. Blood drippin' down my eye.

All by myself an no one there to protect me or nothin. I couldn't really move or run cause I had this heavy book bag full of books.

I never find out who or why.

You don't feel safe at all in school. Only feel safe with a lot of friends. A posse. Watch each other's back.

If you be writin or somethin in the classroom, you gotta watch your back.

Kids set fires in trash cans. Go to library, throw books around. Guns in school cause they scared.

Three guards guard the exits. But they can't be everywhere.

Document 8: The Death Trap of "Fearship"

In his book Street Soldier, *Joe Marshall says that one of the most dangerous problems in a gang is that members begin to confuse friendship with something he calls 'fearship,' a very negative force that is responsible for much of the death and destruction that is associated with gang behavior.*

Our use of the term *fearship* goes along with our rule for living regarding friendship, which identifies a friend as someone who will never lead a friend to danger. When the boys in the 'hood say that they stick together and watch each other's backs and slang and bang and steal and murder for friendship, we maintain that they do it not for friendship but for fearship; that is, out of fear of what their so-called friends are going to think of them or do to them if they don't go along. Fearship is peer pressure at its most destructive.

One of the most vivid cases of fearship I've come across involved an Oakland woman who called [our radio call-in program aimed at gang members] *Street Soldiers* to tell us that she had returned home from work one night to find her fourteen-year-old daughter pointing a shotgun at her. After she wrestled the shotgun away and called the police, she learned that the daughter was trying to join a local Crips set and had been told that to become a member, she would have to kill her mother. The girl was sent to juvenile jail but remained so desperate to join the gang that she wrote her mother requesting that she send a photograph of herself. The mother knew damn well that the girl wanted the picture so that she could show it to her potnas [gang friends] and have *them* kill her. She was forced to go into hiding to escape her own daughter. While the Oakland girl was uncommonly eager to comply with a shockingly heartless demand, it's not uncommon at all for less zealous homies to be driven by fearship to commit murder and mayhem.

Document 9: "Maturing Out" from Gangs

Experts in criminology, law, and social work all have opinions about how the gang culture in our cities can be eradicated. In the following excerpt from his book Wannabe: Gangs in Suburbs and Schools, *Daniel J. Monti discusses his own theory that if gang members are shown believable alternatives to a gang life on the community level, many will adopt those alternatives.*

Well-meaning people in the late nineteenth century invented something called a "settlement house." These houses were put in some of the most troubled neighborhoods that could be found in the cities of their day. Those who ran these places tried to serve as good role models for area residents and to provide services that local folks needed. These settlement houses did not work as well as their founders had hoped, and they certainly did not save all the local residents from their own bad habits or from the poverty that held them tightly. Yet the idea of seeding a troubled neighborhood with individuals and groups committed to staying there and making the place work better had much to recommend it. It still does.

I suggest that the United States already has the manpower and the means to make this work, and much of it is waiting in the several branches of our armed services. Men and women whose careers already have been marked by conspicuous public service await an early retirement as our military establishment is reduced in size. A proposal first made by retired Rear Admiral Norman Johnson of Boston University to put some of these persons to work in old military bases as teachers and mentors to inner-city youngsters has been picked up by other black leaders. This is an excellent idea, but there is no reason why it could not be expanded to make retiring military personnel or police officers full-time residents in troubled neigh-

borhoods and to offer them financial assistance to develop small businesses that will employ many of the youngsters they have helped to train. . . .

What I propose is nothing less than the creation of thousands of settlement houses in the form of these small businesses. The owners would put
persons to work in their own neighborhoods and provide living examples
of competent adults who will not leave the area or tolerate the poor behavior of the youngsters that live there. They also would constitute the first
wave of a home-grown middle class for neighborhoods that other middle-
class minorities have fled. It is unlikely that their presence would inspire
persons who left such neighborhoods to return in large numbers. It is
more likely that the availability of these new role models, middle-class
mentors, or whatever they end up being called, would inspire other people to stay and make the community even more stable. . . .

These new residents and businesses would not eradicate gangs or
employ every young person who could use a job. They would not turn
boys and girls doing bad things into angels. What they probably would do
is curb some gang activities, employ more youngsters in local enterprises,
and command the attention and respect of boys and girls in the area."

Document 10: The Tragic Death of Junior Ragland

*In his article "Gang Intimidation Takes Rising Toll of Court Cases," New York
Times bureau chief Sam Howe Verhovek explains the growing problem of witness intimidation in gang killings. In this section, he describes the frustration of
justice system personnel who cannot protect one of the few witnesses who are willing to step forward.*

Three months after his testimony helped convict a gang member of murder, and just one week before he was to testify in the trial of a second
defendant, 19-year-old Elijah Ragland was found dead in a creek in east
Fort Worth, Texas.

He had been repeatedly shot in the head and neck. And though the
killing in January [1994] remains unsolved, the police say they believe it
was related to Mr. Ragland's testimony.

The police and family members say Mr. Ragland had received several
threats warning him to stay away from the second trial. But Mr. Ragland
was willing to do what an increasing number of witnesses to crimes are
not: testify in court.

Prosecutors around the nation say the intimidation of witnesses, and
their subsequent killing, is on the rise, especially in gang-related crimes.
People who provide investigators with detailed information about crimes
are refusing to divulge the same information in a trial at which they must
publicly face the accused.

In testimony before a Congressional committee, prosecutors in
Washington said the city was failing to pursue 30 to 35 percent of its murder cases because people with knowledge of events refused to cooperate. . . .

In Fort Worth, the unsolved killing of Mr. Ragland has continued to haunt Ms. [Terri] Moore [the former chief prosecutor in the gang unit of the District Attorney's office in Fort Worth]. . . . Tacked on the wall by her desk is a newspaper's small obituary of Mr. Ragland, who, she said, made an agonizing decision to testify in the case of a restaurant owner, Yousef Mirzadeh, who was killed during a holdup. One of the men accused in the killing was Mr. Ragland's brother-in-law.

Speaking of young Mr. Ragland, Ms. Moore said: "Junior just thought it was the right thing to do. It was a horrible crime. A most innocent hard-working person who loved his family tremendously was killed."

And shortly after the trial in which his brother-in-law received a sentence of life in prison, Junior Ragland was dead.

"I used to be able to tell people I never lost a witness," Ms. Moore said, "but I can't say that anymore. It burned me up pretty bad. Now you have to say, 'Yes, you, too, could get killed.'"

Document 11: Mixed Reviews on Death Row Kids' Books

When Stanley "Tookie" Williams was arrested, tried, and convicted in 1981, few believed the powerful gang leader would repent his notorious accomplishment—founding the Crips. However, in 1996 Williams put out a series of children's books aimed at teaching youngsters the folly of gang life. In the following excerpt from Time *magazine, writer James Willwerth examines the evolution of gang killer to children's book writer.*

Williams . . . was condemned to death in 1981 for fatally shotgunning four unresisting victims during motel and convenience-store holdups. But his transformation, he insists, should be judged separately from his crimes. Arriving at San Quentin in 1981 as a feared gangsta godfather, Williams was content for years to watch sullenly from death row as gang violence spread—and with it, an urban nightmare.

Fiercely resistant to authority, Williams spent nearly seven years in solitary confinement and turned to exotic self-help works, including a text on ancient Egyptian philosophy. "I slowly realized I was living a lie," he says. "The respect I cared so much about was based on intimidation, not self-respect. I had been involved in madness." Interviewed in 1993 by author Barbara Cottman Becnel for a history of the Crips and Bloods, Williams asked a favor in return. Becnel carried a videotaped speech by Williams condemning violence to a 1993 gang "summit" in Los Angeles. The audience responded with a standing ovation. Next, Williams told Becnel he wished to write children's books. "I hear this rhetoric about helping one child," he explained. "That's not enough. I wanted to help thousands."

Williams, who has donated his royalties to inner-city activist groups such as Mothers Against Gang Wars, will not discuss his legal future. . . . "I simply don't believe that I'm going to be executed," Williams says calmly. Death-row federal appeals commonly runs a three-to-four-year course, and for Williams, whatever time remains has a clear purpose. "As much as you might want to fit in, don't join a gang," he writes in *Gangs and Wanting to Belong*. "You won't find what you're looking for. All you will find is trouble, pain, and sadness. I know. I did."

Document 12: Teaching Must Be More than a Job

The gang issue is intertwined with the difficulties schools face today. Educators complain that many children do not come to school ready to learn; instead, they are angry and confused, and lack respect for teachers and fellow students. Schools must come to grips with these problems before they can deal effectively with gangs, says former teacher Erlaine Taylor in an excerpt from Carl S. Taylor's Dangerous Society.

There has been a decline in terms of a positive relationship between parents and the school. When I first started teaching the profession was very respected in the community. Students were expected to respect teachers, adults, and the school. Parents were supportive of the teacher at that time. Today it seems that many parents don't care. In return teachers have changed—many young teachers are responding to the negatives.

Television, the excitement, pimps, prostitutes, sports people, are the images the children are exposed to day in and day out. It's very frustrating to see the decline of so many young children. Education has such a limited appeal to many parents and students. It's as if they resent education; there's a subtle feeling that educators are elite. The lure of the streets is stronger than ever. When young children see expensive cars and clothes that cost more than those of their parents, teachers, principals, or anyone else in the community, they believe that this is correct. American leaders are not reflecting qualities of brotherly love. Success is money and power. . . . These children are acting out the violence and cruelty that their parents and leaders have displayed. Their home life is shot, no love, violence, and cruelty. So it's no wonder that they come to school ready to hurt someone. It's very hard to teach under that type of pressure. The teaching profession has felt the pressure and burden of the changed student. Some teachers have developed the attitude of "it's a job. I got mine, you can get yours."

We must do something real soon. . . . It's not only the kids engaged in criminal activities but the whole community suffers.

STUDY QUESTIONS

Chapter 1

1. In your opinion, is the use of the term *savagery* excessive in describing gang violence? Why or why not? What is the "illogical turnabout" that Rafael, the young boy from Richmond, California, makes in his thinking about violence and joining a gang?

2. In Viewpoint 2, gang counselor Lou Williams says that many so-called gang members are "just little babies . . . playing, dressing up, talking the talk, pretending to be something they're not." Why does this irritate him? Why does the author of this viewpoint think that society should be concerned about these youth? Would the author of Viewpoint 1 agree?

3. What changes in American society have encouraged gang infiltration of the workplace, according to Viewpoint 3? What could account for the rising presence of gangs in the military? How would the author of Viewpoint 2 explain the increased presence of gangs in these two areas?

4. In your opinion, do the gangs mentiond in Viewpoint 4, Bay Boys and the Double-Nine Crew, fit the definition of a gang? Why or why not? Is the usage of the term *gang* consistent in Viewpoints 1, 2, 3, and 4?

Chapter 2

1. The lack of supportive fathers is often cited as the reason that young people join gangs. Some, however, have called this thinking sexist, because it implies that women alone cannot adequately nurture their own children. Do you agree? Why or why not?

2. How does the kind of respect mentioned by Twace in Viewpoint 2 differ from that mentioned by Joe Marshall in the same viewpoint?

3. Dickie and Rodney, two of the young men interviewed by Carl Taylor in Viewpoint 3, have strong negative reactions to the idea of working at a "regular job." Can you understand their feelings? What, in your opinion, could motivate them to change their thinking about jobs?

Chapter 3

1. The author of Viewpoint 1 complains that gang members are less likely to be punished for often horrendous crimes than others.

Why? In your opinion, would trying juveniles as adults in such crimes be a workable option? Explain your reasoning.

2. Writer Luis Rodriguez and others feel strongly that gangs can contribute to society by the very characteristics that make them seem dangerous, especially by "warrior energy." What is warrior energy, and why does Rodriguez say it is positive? Would the author of Viewpoint 1 agree?

3. How distinct are the opinions of Luis Rodriguez and Father Greg Boyle in their view of gang behavior? Would the author of Viewpoint 1 support programs such as In My Shoes? Explain your answer.

4. The author of Viewpoint 4 urges school faculty and administrators to welcome gang members into their schools and "to validate them as people." In your opinion, can this be accomplished without endangering non–gang member students? Should gang status be considered by school personnel in their dealings with students?

For Further Reading

Leon Bing, *Do or Die*. New York: HarperCollins, 1991. Very readable text with helpful quotations.

Charles Patrick Ewing, *Kids Who Kill*. New York: Free Press, 1990. Chilling accounts, but fascinating reading. Good information on the role of family in youth violence.

Keith Elliot Greenberg, *Out of the Gang*. Minneapolis: Lerner Publications, 1992. Interesting reading, good section on peer pressure and gangs.

Joan Nordquist, ed., *Violence in American Society: A Bibliography*. Santa Cruz, CA: Reference and Research Services, 1994. Extremely helpful.

Roger Rosen and Patra McSharry, eds., *Street Gangs: Gaining Turf, Losing Ground*. New York: Rosen, 1991. Good information on how the community suffers when gangs thrive.

Evan Stark, *Everything You Need to Know About Street Gangs*. New York: Rosen, 1995. Highly readable text; good bibliography.

Margi Trapani, *Working Together Against Gang Violence*. New York: Rosen, 1996. Easy reading; helpful section on strategies for community awareness.

WORKS CONSULTED

Books

Celeste Fremon, *Father Greg and the Homeboys*. Westport, CT: Hyperion, 1995. Takes the position that organized churches' approach to youth violence has failed.

Sandra Gardner, *Street Gangs in America*. New York: Franklin Watts, 1992. Very readable; excellent bibliography and endnotes.

Debra Goldentyer, *Gangs*. Austin, TX: Steck-Vaughn, 1994. Very readable text, good photographs.

Susan Goodwillie, ed., *Voices from the Future: Our Children Tell Us About Violence in America*. New York: Crown, 1993. Excellent variety of one-on-one interviews with teenagers. Powerful photographs.

JoAnn Bren Guernsey, *Youth Violence: An Americam Epidemic?* Minneapolis: Lerner, 1996. Excellent chapter on violence in American culture.

James Haskins, *Street Gangs: Yesterday and Today*. New York: Hastings House, 1974. Fascinating information, especially on early gang attire and fighting styles.

Allan M. Hoffman and Randal Summers, eds., *Schools, Violence, and Society*. Westport, CT: Praeger, 1996. Good data on gang violence in schools; helpful bibliography.

Malcolm W. Klein, *The American Street Gang: Its Nature, Prevalence, and Control*. New York: Oxford University Press, 1995. Difficult reading, but good, scholarly research on American gangs and their development through the last fifty years.

Shirley R. Lal, Dhyan Lal, and Charles M. Achilles, *Handbook on Gangs in Schools: Strategies to Reduce Gang-Related Activities*. Thousand Oaks, CA: Corwin Press, 1993. Helpful information on changing presence of gangs in public schools.

Ann Lawson, *Kids & Gangs: What Parents and Educators Need to Know*. Minneapolis: Johnson Institute, 1994. Concise introduction to various kinds of American street gangs. Good section on parenting styles that increase likelihood of gang affiliation.

Joseph Marshall, *Street Soldier: One Man's Struggle to Save a Generation*. New York: Delacorte, 1996. Very valuable account of the gang situation in California by an activist insider.

Daniel J. Monti, *Wannabe: Gangs in Suburbs and Schools*. Cambridge, MA: Blackwell, 1994. Readable account; well documented.

Karen Osman, *Gangs*. San Diego: Lucent Books, 1992. Good glossary and index; excellent chapter on tagging.

Earl Shorris, *Latinos: A Biography of the People*. New York: W.W. Norton, 1992. Somewhat difficult reading, but excellent material on violence in the Latino community.

Ben Sonder, *Gangs*. New York: Benchmark Books, 1996. Good section on vendettas, well illustrated with black-and-white photographs.

Irving A. Spergel, *The Youth Gang Problem: A Community Approach*. New York: Oxford University Press, 1995. Good sections on the role of schools in solving the gang problem.

Gail B. Stewart, *Gangs*. San Diego: Lucent Books, 1997. Very readable account of a girl gang member.

Carl S. Taylor, *Dangerous Society*. East Lansing: Michigan State University Press, 1990. Graphic yet intriguing quotations from gang members on a wide variety of subjects.

Periodicals

Jordan Bonfante, "Entrepreneurs of Crack," *Time*, February 27, 1995, pp. 22–23.

Greg Boyle, interviewed by Sharon R. Bard, "Gang Life," *Creation Spirituality*, Spring 1994, p. 21.

Douglas A. Clay and Frank D. Aquila, "'Spittin' the Lit'—Fact or Fad? Gangs and America's Schools," *Phi Delta Kappan*, September 1994, pp. 65–68.

Lewis Cole, "Hyper Violence," *Rolling Stone*, December 1, 1994. pp. 106ff.

Laron Davis, "In the Mind of a True Disciple," *Prison Life*, March 1995, p. 46.

Elisabeth Dunham, "Bad Girls: Four Real-Life Girl Gansters Speak Out," *Teen*, August 1995, pp. 52ff.

Economist, "Gangs in the Heartland," May 25, 1996, p. 29.

Celeste Fremon, "Tough Love," *Utne Reader*, March/April 1996, pp. 95–100.

Michael Goodman, "Coastal Nostra," *Los Angeles Magazine*, June 1996, pp. 72ff.

Chris Gravesi, "I Just Want My Baby's Killer Found," *Minneapolis Star Tribune*, July 23, 1996, p. 1A.

Samuel Greengard, "Have Gangs Invaded Your Workplace?" *Personnel Journal*, February 1996, pp. 46–54.

Edward Humes, "Can a Gang Girl Go Straight?" *Glamour*, March 1996, pp. 212ff.

Ice-T, "To Live and Die in LA," *Playboy*, February 1994, p. 62ff.

Robert Koehler, "Scared Straighter," *Chicago*, February 1997, p. 20.

Albert McGee, "Ridin' Under the Five-Pointed Star," *Prison Life*, March 1995, p. 50.

Adam Miller, "Gang Murder in the Heartland," *Rolling Stone*, February 22, 1996, pp. 48ff.

Victoria Pope, "Crack Invades a Small Town," *U.S. News & World Report*, April 22, 1996, pp. 34–43.

Luis J. Rodriguez, "Rekindling the Warrior," *Utne Reader*, July/August 1994, pp. 58–59.

Nancy Jo Sales, "Teenage Gangland," *New York*, December 16, 1996, pp. 32–39.

Thomas Toch, "When Killers Come to Class: Violence in Schools," *U.S. News & World Report*, November 8, 1993, pp. 16–23.

Sam Howe Verhovek, "Gang Intimidation Takes Rising Toll of Court Cases," *New York Times*, October 7, 1994, p. 16.

Gregory Vistica, 'Gangstas' in the Ranks," *Newsweek*, July 24, 1995, p. 48.

James Willwerth, "Lessons Learned on Death Row," *Time*, September 23, 1996.

Gordon Witkin, "Enlisting the Feds in the War on Gangs," *U.S. News & World Report*, March 6, 1995, pp. 38–40.

INDEX

ABOUT THE AUTHOR

Gail B. Stewart is the author of more than eighty books for children and young adults. She lives in Minneapolis, Minnesota, with her husband Carl and their sons Ted, Eliot, and Flynn. When she is not writing, she spends her time reading, walking, and watching her sons play soccer.